T0114108

Cambridge Elements ≡

Elements in Phonetics
edited by
David Deterding
Universiti Brunei Darussalam

SPONTANEOUS SPEECH

Benjamin V. Tucker
*University of Alberta
and Northern Arizona University*

Yoichi Mukai
*Vancouver Island University
and University of Alberta*

CAMBRIDGE
UNIVERSITY PRESS

CAMBRIDGE
UNIVERSITY PRESS

Shaftesbury Road, Cambridge CB2 8EA, United Kingdom

One Liberty Plaza, 20th Floor, New York, NY 10006, USA

477 Williamstown Road, Port Melbourne, VIC 3207, Australia

314–321, 3rd Floor, Plot 3, Splendor Forum, Jasola District Centre,
New Delhi – 110025, India

103 Penang Road, #05–06/07, Visioncrest Commercial, Singapore 238467

Cambridge University Press is part Cambridge University Press & Assessment, a
department of the University of Cambridge.

We share the University's mission to contribute to society through the pursuit of
education, learning and research at the highest international levels of excellence.

www.cambridge.org
Information on this title: www.cambridge.org/9781108932004
DOI: 10.1017/9781108943024

First published 2023

A catalogue record for this publication is available from the British Library.

ISBN 978-1-108-93200-4 Paperback
ISSN 2634-1689 (online)
ISSN 2634-1670 (print)

Additional resources for this publication at
www.cambridge.org/tucker_supplementary.

Cambridge University Press & Assessment has no responsibility for the persistence
or accuracy of
URLs for external or third-party internet websites referred to in this publication
and does not guarantee that any content on such websites is, or will remain,
accurate or appropriate.

Spontaneous Speech

Elements in Phonetics

DOI: 10.1017/9781108943024
First published online: January 2023

Benjamin V. Tucker
University of Alberta and Northern Arizona University

Yoichi Mukai
Vancouver Island University and University of Alberta

Author for correspondence: Benjamin V. Tucker, bvtucker@ualberta.ca

Abstract: Phonetic research investigates how speakers and listeners use speech to convey messages. The speech produced to encode a particular message can vary wildly. Understanding and explaining the phonetic variability embodied in this example is one of the main motivations for this Element. Why and how do speakers produce this variability and how does it impact listeners? This Element focuses on spontaneous speech and its relationship with phonetic research. The authors discuss background and describe research investigating the variation that occurs when speakers and listeners are engaged in spontaneous, conversational speech. As a result, this Element explores aspects of spontaneous speech from the phonetic perspective using both production and perception areas of phonetics.

Keywords: spontaneous speech, reduction, speech production, speech perception, phonetics

Supplementary material for this Element can be found at:
www.cambridge.org/tucker_supplementary

ISBNs: 9781108932004 (PB), 9781108943024 (OC)
ISSNs: 2634-1689 (online), 2634-1670 (print)

Contents

1 Introduction

Phonetic research investigates how speakers and listeners use speech to communicate. Speech produced to encode a particular message varies wildly; this is called phonetic variability. Consider, for example, the comic in Figure 1, in which Earl says *Jeet yet?* [dʒit jɛt] or *Did you eat yet?* This could also have been produced as [dɪdʒu it jɛt]. Why did Earl say [dɪdʒu it jɛt], and how is it that Clyde understands this message and responds in a similar way? Understanding and explaining the phonetic variability in spontaneous speech, as found in the comic (Figure 1), is the main motivation for the present overview.

In spontaneous speech, the realization of syllables and segments in words is highly variable (e.g., Greenberg, 1999; Hawkins, 2003; Ernestus and Warner, 2011), as illustrated by the example in the preceding paragraph. Previous work has found that 54 percent of words in the Corpus of Conversational American English (Pitt et al., 2007) were realized in variable forms, and 25 percent of these forms were missing a segment when the produced form was compared to a dictionary transcription of the word (Johnson, 2004; Dilts, 2013). Maekawa (2005) found in the Corpus of Spontaneous Japanese (Maekawa, 2003) that 20 percent of type tokens include pronunciation variants, and the occurrence ratio of these variants differs depending on speech style. In this Element, we explore the variability found in the production of spontaneous speech and its impact on speech perception.

A major part of the variability in spontaneous speech is described as phonetic reduction. That is, speech which is realized with shortening, deletion, and/or incomplete articulation of segments (Pols, 1996; Greenberg, 1999; Warner and Tucker, 2011) in comparison to a dictionary entry of the word's pronunciation. For example, in English, *Do you have to* was realized as [dætə] (audio file below) (Warner and Tucker, 2011), in Japanese, 少し話して *sukoshi hanashite* 'speak a little bit' /sɯkoʃihanaʃite/ was realized as [sɯkoʃanaʃite] (Arai, 1999) (the high front vowel and glottal fricative [ih] are assimilated to

Figure 1 An illustration of reduction. *Pickles* January 2, 2003. Used by permission from the *Washington Post*.

Sound 1 Audio file available at
www.cambridge.org/Tucker_do_you_have_to_short

the preceding post-alveolar fricative), and in Dutch, words like *mogelijk* 'possible' /moːɣələk/ are produced as /mok/ in spontaneous speech (Keune et al., 2005). For the interested reader, we have created a web page that exemplifies these types of reduction in a variety of languages. Audio examples of reductions can be found here: www.cambridge.org/tucker_supplementary. Phonetic variability, including reduction, in spontaneous speech is investigated with the goal to understand the governing articulatory and perceptual constraints (e.g., Lindblom, 1990). Despite the existing phonetic research, there remains much that is not understood about how variation is realized in spontaneous speech. In the sections that follow, we explore what is known about this variability.

William Labov, when describing the Observer's Paradox, summarizes well one of the reasons why spontaneous speech is important: "To obtain the data most important for linguistic theory, we have to observe how people speak when they are not being observed" (Labov, 1972, p. 113).

One of the primary arguments for investigating spontaneous speech is that it samples a central part of the vast array of speech types that speakers and listeners use for communication. As noted in Wagner et al. (2015), it is important to investigate a range of speech styles, including spontaneous speech. If the goal is to understand communication from the perspective of ecological validity (i.e., a sample that reflects actual speaker and listener experience), then it is important to understand how this range of speech types impacts speech production and perception.

In the rest of the introductory section, we define the key terms and discuss the major conceptual topics and questions around spontaneous speech. We then describe a few of the domains in which spontaneous speech has been investigated. These introductory sections are followed by sections describing the most important findings in the areas of production and perception as they pertain to spontaneous speech.

1.1 What Is Spontaneous Speech?

Spontaneous speech is a cover term for many different speech styles (Coupland, 2007). We define speech style as the form of language produced on the basis of internal and external factors. These factors could depend on situation, formality, mood, individual choice, and environment. Spontaneous speech as a speech style includes conversational, connected, casual, fast, natural, and vernacular speech. It can be contrasted with careful, read, laboratory speech, and other terms that have been applied to careful types of speech. Careful types of speech also refer to a range of different tasks and styles, such as scripted, careful, and formal speech, which may include a speaker reading a list of words, a participant naming a set of pictures, and a reporter reading a news report.

The terminology around speech style and spontaneous speech is problematic as there is no agreed taxonomy of speech style. As a result, researchers may use the same terms for different speech styles. For example, they could refer to 'connected' speech in describing their speech material. In one case this could mean carefully read sentences, while in another case this could mean a conversation between two speakers. Further, determining what is and is not spontaneous is difficult. For example, a politician giving a prepared speech or an actor rehearsing a script produces speech that is meant to be similar to spontaneous speech but is not spontaneous. What makes spontaneous speech *spontaneous* is the fact that it is not prepared. As a result, even though a political speech or an acted conversation sounds "natural," it does not make that speech spontaneous. This draws a distinction between speech that is connected but prepared, and spontaneous speech that is connected but not prepared.

To better illustrate this issue, Figure 2a demonstrates the dynamics of speech style with three hypothesized dimensions in a multidimensional, multimodal space of speech (adapted from ideas presented in Tucker, 2007; Warner, 2011). (Please note that the values and dimensions assigned here are arbitrary and are simply meant as an illustration.) We use speech style to cover a wide range of possible speech types or genres. The multidimensional space represents three continua: (1) careful to casual speech (labelled Careful), (2) fast to slow (Rate), and (3) reduced to unreduced (Reduction). Careful, our first dimension, is described as hyper-articulated speech and holds one end of our Careful continuum. Careful speech may be hyper-articulated, and a speaker is more likely to pay attention to how they are speaking. The other end of the continuum, casual speech, can also be referred to as hypo-articulated or conversational speech (Lindblom, 1990). In comparison to careful speech, casual speech tends to exhibit a higher articulation rate, lower fundamental frequency (F0 or the frequency of vocal fold vibration) variation and declination, more frequent hesitations, approximated articulation, and shorter segment duration and prosodic units (e.g., Mehta and Cutler, 1988; Laan, 1997; Cutler, 1998).

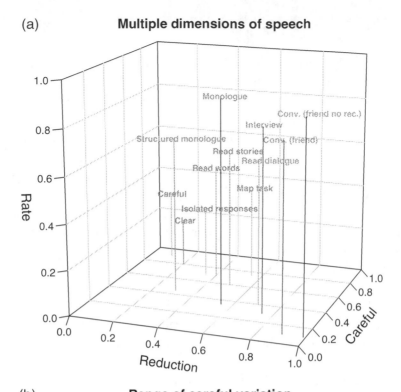

(a) **Multiple dimensions of speech**

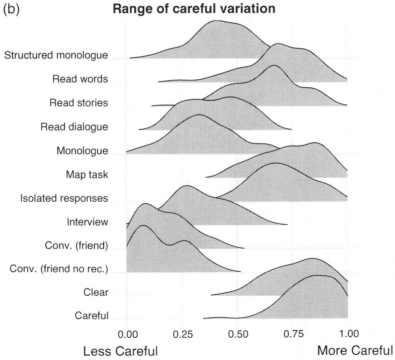

(b) **Range of careful variation**

Figure 2 (a) Illustration of a three-dimensional space of possible ranges of speech variation. (b) Illustration of the range of variability and overlap possible within a dimension.

The other dimensions of Figure 2a include Rate and Reduction. Rate is meant to represent a generic range from slow to fast speech. While there are dependencies between our three dimensions, they can also vary independently. For example, conversational speech with a friend can range from slow to fast depending on external influences such as topic and emphasis. For Reduction, the generic range includes extreme examples of reduction like in the example of *jeet yet?* at the reduced end (from Figure 1). The unreduced end of the range might include *did you eat yet?*, with emphasis placed on each word. In the case of strengthening or enhancement, at the careful end of the Reduction range, speakers produce segments with longer durations or with increased articulatory precision. Figure 2b illustrates that it is also possible for a type of speech to vary (e.g., read or laboratory speech), as noted in our rate example. In other words, read speech does not exist as a single point on the careful dimension in our multidimensional space. It ranges depending on a number of circumstances. Figure 2b is also meant to illustrate that speech types might be thought of as overlapping distributions along the represented dimensions as opposed to static points.

While acknowledging that spontaneous speech is a cover term including many types of speech, we attempt to provide an inclusive definition. According to Beckman (1997), spontaneous speech is 'not read speech'. In Warner (2012), spontaneous speech is 'nothing read', adding noncareful speech. Warner (2012) also includes speech from structured tasks such as monologues or Map Tasks (described in Section 2) as spontaneous speech. In both cases, *not read* is the defining characteristic of spontaneous speech. However, this does not include other tasks that are not read but also are not spontaneous, such as picture naming or repetition. We propose the following working definition: Spontaneous speech is speech produced by a speaker in an informal, dynamic, unrehearsed, casual manner.

Researchers dichotomize variables of interest and contrast theories and methodologies against one another. For example, it is frequently the case that spontaneous speech is set in contrast to laboratory speech. They may even interpret the recent emphasis or increase in research on spontaneous speech as ignoring or belittling work using laboratory speech. It is important to remember that all speech styles are important, and laboratory-recorded speech styles are also a crucial part of speech research (see also Xu, 2010; Wagner et al., 2015).

In research using spontaneous speech – particularly studies that compare spontaneous and laboratory speech – the word 'canonical' is used. Traditionally, the canonical form is thought of as the careful or laboratory production of the word. This is the same version of the word that would be found in a standard dictionary. Cangemi and Niebuhr (2018) define the canonical form as: "symbolic, linear, and minimalistically contrastive representations, as in the case of phonological transcriptions of words."

When investigating spontaneous speech, the canonical form is used as a standard of comparison (like comparing the canonical form to spontaneous speech) to indicate if there is variation in the form of reduction (e.g., deletion) or strengthening (e.g., epenthesis) in the speech. When doing this kind of comparison, a question arises with regard to what the appropriate canonical form is and who decides what it is. In large part, this is influenced by the orthography or the assumed 'phonological representation'. However, investigation of spontaneous speech has found that the canonical form is infrequently produced (e.g., Dilts, 2013). For example, Greenberg (1999) reports eighty-seven different pronunciations of the word *and* in the four hours of the Switchboard Transcription Corpus (Godfrey et al., 1992; Greenberg et al., 1996). The 'canonical' form [ænd] is produced 11 times out of 521 instances, while the form [æn] is the most common. There are advantages to making reference to a canonical form, especially when a researcher is attempting to define reduction or strengthening from a point of comparison (Cangemi and Niebuhr, 2018). However, using the canonical form is problematic when this is assumed to be the form that the speaker/listener stores as part of their lexical representation. If we were to assume that the canonical form of *and* [ænd] was the most common form and all other variant forms were reductions, then the conclusion based on the distribution of pronunciations in Switchboard reported by Greenberg (1999) would be that nearly 98 percent of the forms produced are 'reduced'.

As a result, the term 'canonical' should be used with care because it oversimplifies a complex process and likely misrepresents what is produced in spontaneous speech. Canonical is used for a pseudo representation of what a really careful pronunciation is or what the dictionary says the *proper* pronunciation is. If we, however, focus not on reduction or strengthening but on the variation of the forms produced, we will likely find that the most common form offers production and processing advantages (as we see in the discussion of the literature that follows) and that disadvantages are found for the less-common-reduced and extremely careful forms. For more information on the canonical form, Cangemi and Niebuhr (2018) provide a historical context for the use of the canonical form in linguistics and discuss in detail the advantages and disadvantages of making use of the canonical form for speech research.

1.2 Domains of Spontaneous Speech Research

Thus far, we have discussed spontaneous speech from the phonetic sciences perspective. We continue to do this throughout this Element; however, we also mention other areas that investigate spontaneous speech. For example, in sociolinguistics, what we have called spontaneous speech – or speech in its natural setting – is the central type of speech studied (Kendall and Fridland, 2021). Sociolinguists and sociophoneticians have long been interested in speech style (Coupland, 2007; Schilling, 2013). In addition, spontaneous speech is a central part in discourse studies, with research focusing on topics such as spoken interaction and conversation analysis (Hymes, 1962; Local et al., 1986; Renkema, 2009; Renkema and Schubert, 2018).

Another area where spontaneous speech plays an important role is language acquisition. In particular, spontaneous speech is used to investigate what infants and children hear and produce as they learn language. In these instances, researchers make written or audio recordings of what was said to and around the child or what the child said. They utilize these data to investigate aspects and processes of language learning (Braunwald and Brislin, 1979; Tomasello and Stahl, 2004). For example, the LENA (**L**anguage **En**vironment **A**nalysis) system is a recorder that is placed in a vest worn by the child and records language input and output (e.g., VanDam et al., 2016).

In what is now classical work on speech errors, Meringer and Mayer (1895) listened to spontaneous conversations and recorded the errors produced by speakers. For example, a speaker may produce *coy tar* instead of *toy car*. This initial article has led to many publications on speech errors in linguistics and speech production (e.g., Fromkin, 1971, 1984; Frisch and Wright, 2002; Alderete et al., 2021). Early speech error results have been used as evidence for linguistic structure, such as phonemes (speech sounds) and morphemes (parts of a word), and also used as the basis of many of the early speech production models (Fromkin, 1971; Garrett, 1975). While subsequent research has found ways to experimentally elicit speech errors, it is still dominated by recording and analyzing spontaneous speech.

Spontaneous speech has also played a role in speech technology. The production and recognition of fluent spontaneous speech is the target of many speech technology applications. While synthesizing spontaneous speech in a fluent manner has been shown to be difficult (Shriberg, 2005), recent successes with deep neural networks seem to have overcome many of the challenges (e.g., van den Oord et al., 2016). In addition, automatic speech recognition has struggled with recognizing spontaneous speech (Ward, 1989; Shriberg, 2005), but the recent advent of deep neural networks in recognition has advanced the field tremendously (e.g., Hannun et al., 2014). While these methods have made major headway in the area of dealing with spontaneous speech and automatic speech recognition in general, the reductions that occur in spontaneous speech still pose a challenge for many automatic speech recognition systems.

The desire to provide better solutions to challenges in speech technology has generated related phonetic research on spontaneous speech. At the same time, the development of spontaneous speech resources has complemented and contributed to phonetic investigation. For example, some of the earliest corpora (a collection of linguistic material) of spontaneous speech (e.g., Zue et al., 1990; Godfrey et al., 1992) were developed for the purpose of improving speech technology. While the focus of these corpora was on speech technology, the corpora also provided new data for phonetic research.

In the next two sections, we describe phonetic research in production and perception involving spontaneous speech. In the description of the findings in Section 2, there are types of spontaneous speech that we have not pursued in this Element. One example of this is investigation of clear speech. Clear speech is spontaneously produced and is an attempt by the speaker to increase the speech intelligibility (make the speech more understandable) in challenging situations. For example, this includes changes made to speech when talking to a non-native speaker or in noise, and it can be considered a type of enhancement. There is an abundance of research on clear speech, and we encourage interested readers to use the citations provided in this paragraph as a starting point (e.g., Bradlow and Bent, 2002; Smiljanić and Bradlow, 2005; Uchanski, 2005; Ferguson and Kewley-Port, 2007).

We divide the investigation of spontaneous speech into the two major branches of phonetic research: production and perception. In each section, we provide a brief overview of theories and models. We also provide an overview of methods used in spontaneous speech. While we have divided the research into production and perception, it is important to be aware that understanding one is important for understanding the other. As a result, a subset of the studies described investigated both production and perception. Sections 2 and 3 provide an overview of relevant findings and a starting place to learn more about these topics.

2 Production

Investigation of speech production started with observational reports and counts of phenomena of interest (e.g., speech errors). While these methods are still used, much of the current phonetic research focuses on the acoustic analysis of spontaneous speech. In the remainder of this section, we describe models and theories of spontaneous speech production, methods for the collection of spontaneous speech data, variability in the signal, effects of context, and disfluencies in spontaneous speech.

2.1 Models and Theories

Models of speech production focusing on the cognitive aspects of speech start with the semantic intent (what the speaker wants to say) and end with an abstract phonological representation (often the phoneme but occasionally other representations). Weaver++ (Levelt, 1999) and Dell's Neural Network model (1999) are examples of cognitive preparation models and they allow researchers to connect cognitive aspects of speech production with the phonological output. Detailed overviews of cognitive preparation models of speech production can be found in Clifton et al. (2013), Harley (2013), Stemberger (2017), and Zwitserlood (2018). Because these models stop at the level of the phoneme, they do not make predictions about the production of spontaneous speech. However, they are important and can be extended if a researcher interested in spontaneous speech wants to connect cognitive processes to variability in spontaneous speech.

There are also models of speech production that focus on motor preparation. They take the abstract phonological representation and generate a sequence of articulatory events, which can make predictions about variability in spontaneous speech. These models are concerned with the timing of articulatory gestures. Models such as Task Dynamics (Saltzman and Munhall, 1989) and Articulatory Phonology (Browman and Goldstein, 1992) focus on issues of how speech sounds are sequenced.

Finally, models of motor execution focus on the execution of the articulatory events resulting in an acoustic signal, such as Tube Talker (Story, 2005), Vocal Tract Lab (Birkholz et al., 2006), and DIVA (Guenther, 2016; DIVA does both preparation and execution).

All three of these types of models (cognitive, motor preparation, and motor execution) are necessary to model speech production. There have been a few attempts to join these separate models to create a 'full' model of speech production (Hickok, 2014b; Rapp et al., 2014; Roelofs, 2014). These joint models allow researchers to connect cognitive processes to articulatory and acoustic events. Models of cognitive preparation and motor preparation focus on the production of single words. As a result, they are not able to deal with larger contextual effects of spontaneous speech.

These models include both conceptual and computational implementations. The conceptual models can produce hypotheses and predictions, though there still remains a lot of leeway in their interpretation, while computational models attempt to simulate the process. This simulated process allows computational models to make specific predictions, guiding the researchers to make specific changes to the model so that they can observe whether the outcome of these changes mirrors what happens in experimental data. Computational models like DIVA are extremely useful as it is possible to try and simulate the variability that occurs in spontaneous speech.

The Hypo- and Hyper-articulation theory (Lindblom, 1990), known as H&H theory, represents a theoretical framework that accounts for the inherent variability in speech production. In this framework, Lindblom (1990) proposes that speakers modify their speech on a continuum based on situational demands to maximize communicative efficiency. Thus, a speaker will try to find the most efficient way to say something while making sure that the listener is able to understand the message. For example, a speaker will talk in a relatively casual manner when talking to a friend in a quiet room; however, when they are attending a noisy gathering, the speech is modified (e.g., increased amplitude, longer segment durations, slower speech rate) to account for the additional noise introduced by the gathering.

Researchers have treated communication as an information stream and utilize various measures of predictability to form their explanation of variability. These ideas come from aspects of Zipf's Principle of Least Effort (Zipf, 1949) and Shannon's mathematical theory of communication (Shannon, 1948). Along these lines, van Son et al. (1998) propose the principle of *efficient communication* and Aylett and Turk (2004, 2006) propose the Smooth Signal Redundancy Hypothesis. Both seek to balance the information flow and production in attempting to account for the variability in spontaneous speech. The Probabilistic Reduction Hypothesis (Jurafsky et al., 2001; Bell et al., 2009) indicates that speech is more likely to be reduced when it occurs in more probable situations. Jaeger and Buz (2017) and Cohen Priva and Jaeger (2018) have expanded these ideas of probabilistic reduction. In spontaneous speech, there are also instances where enhancement, instead of reduction, occurs as a result of high probability. Predictability can be calculated in many different ways and for different components of language. As a result, these different types of predictability reflect different aspects of communication. Kuperman et al. (2007) (discussed in more detail in Section 2.4) find enhancement of compound interfixes in Dutch when they are predictable from the morphological context as opposed to sequence predictability. As a result, they propose the Paradigmatic Signal Enhancement Hypothesis to account for instances of enhancement, which likely occur in concert with the other instances of reduction (Cohen, 2015; Sims, 2016; Tucker et al., 2019b; Tomaschek et al., 2021a, 2021b).

2.2 Research Methods

In this section, we discuss relevant methods for the investigation of spontaneous speech, but we also refer the interested reader to Warner (2012), who has written a chapter on this topic. Because of recent computational advancement, a variety of types of corpus data has been developed in various languages, and the use of corpora has become a prominent method in the investigation of spontaneous speech. An example of a spontaneous American English speech corpus is the Switchboard Corpus (Godfrey et al., 1992), which is also a commonly used corpus for training of applications in speech technology. The corpus was collected by recording several minutes of short telephone conversations from over 500 participants. Fifty of these speakers recorded over an hour of speech. These recordings are accompanied by time-aligned word boundaries and word-level transcription. Another English corpus is the Buckeye Corpus of conversational speech (Pitt et al., 2007). This corpus used sociolinguistic interview speech, where a researcher elicits speech from a participant by asking questions in such a way that the participant does most of the talking. These recordings were subsequently time-aligned at the word and phone levels using a forced-alignment system. The Corpus of Spontaneous Japanese (Maekawa, 2003) recorded four different speech styles: academic presentation, simulated public speech, dialogue, and read speech. The academic presentation comprises live recordings of academic talks, and the simulated public speech includes studio recordings of casual speech presented in front of a small audience in a relatively relaxed atmosphere. Dialogue is composed of interviews, task-oriented dialogue, and free dialogue. For the read speech, transcriptions of the academic presentation were read by the same speaker. This corpus also contains word- and phoneme-level alignment. The Kiel Corpus of Spoken German (Kohler, 1996; Kohler et al., 2018) contains both read and spontaneous speech. These data have been generated by asking participants to read short stories, and the spontaneous speech was generated via task-based scenarios designed to elicit spontaneous speech from the participants. The corpus contains time-aligned phonemic transcription and prosodic labelling. The Karl Eberhards Korpus (Arnold and Tomaschek, 2016) contains dialogues of southern German. For this corpus, pairs of participants who know each other conducted a simulated telephone call together, each of them was seated in a separate booth and they could hear each other over the headphones. Interestingly, twenty of the participants were also recorded using electromagnetic articulography, which recorded points on their lips and tongue during speech. Warner and Tucker (2011) collected spontaneous speech by placing participants in a sound-attenuated booth and asking them to call a close friend or family member. A separate head-mounted microphone was placed over the participants' ear for recording purposes. In this way, the participants speak with someone they know well and the speaking partner is not being recorded, helping the participants relax and focus on the conversation, encouraging them to speak in a more natural way. These are a few of the corpora of spontaneous speech that are publicly available. There are also resources designed to help researchers identify new corpora (e.g., `slrb.net`, `talkbank.org`, and `ldc.upen.edu`).

One of the major disadvantages of using a corpus of spontaneous speech is that the experimenter has little control over what is being said, with the result that a particular phone (i.e., speech sound) or word of interest might not occur or be produced rarely in a particular conversation (Fowler and Housum, 1987). More controlled methods involve asking participants to complete cooperative communication tasks, as in summarizing an image or film. For such tasks, variations on the Map Task are commonly used (e.g., Brown et al., 1985; Anderson et al., 1991; Van Engen et al., 2010; Baker and Hazan, 2011). In the Map Task, pairs of participants are asked to navigate from one point on a map to another point following a path that is only shown in the map of one of the participants. A variation on this task is the spot the difference or Diapix task (Van Engen et al., 2010), where two participants have similar pictures and they have to determine what the differences are in the images. For example, in Figure 3, we have created a basic version of a simple spot the difference task. Figure 3b does not have a *fox*, and some other items are also missing. In this case, both participants are going to produce the word *fox* at least once but most likely several times in the course of the task, providing consistency and repetition for subsequent analysis. The disadvantage with these tasks is that one might argue that using a controlled task restricts the spontaneity of the speech.

Corpora can also be created using existing recordings of speech. The Red Hen Archive (Steen and Turner, 2021) is an excellent example of this type of resource. The archive is a compilation of news and media from television, and on average 150 hours of new material is added each day. While much of the speech recorded is read speech (e.g., news reports), other portions vary in spontaneity, including interviews, discussions, and debates. Another example of a corpus compiled using existing recordings is the research by Sonderegger et al. (2017), which analyzed data from a season of the Big Brother UK television show. In these data, there are recordings of participant interactions, individual monologues, and responses to questions.

While these methods come with distinct advantages, as they are a relatively simple way to access lots of data, sorting through so much data and making use of it can be a daunting challenge. In addition, from an acoustic point of view, there are several potential challenges with this type of data. It is possible that digital media has been compressed (e.g., MP3), which impacts the quality of the recorded material, limiting the types of acoustic analyses that can be performed (Gonzalez et al., 2003; Fuchs and Maxwell, 2016). The recording situations also vary for the different programs. For instance, the characteristics

(a)

(b)

Figure 3 Example spot the difference task. Image credit M. J. Tucker.

of the microphones may vary, and the distance between the speaker's mouth and the microphone may also vary (Jannetts et al., 2019). These differences impact measures of loudness, and such differences may occur within a single participant or within a specific show, resulting in unintended variation in the speech. However, the advantage of being able to analyze such large sets of data from individual speakers may outweigh the challenges associated with this type of data, as long as the researcher takes the disadvantages into account.

Forced alignment is an automatic process in which a computer takes a recording and transcript of the recording and provides a time-aligned file indicating phone and word boundaries. The aligner does this by 'looking up' the pronunciation of a word in a dictionary (a list of orthographic words paired with a phonemic transcription) and then attempts to align the set of phones provided by the dictionary entry to the acoustic signal using pretrained acoustic models. The transcription in the dictionary generally conforms with the canonical form but additional forms can be added (e.g., the dictionary could include [ænd] and [æn]). Forced alignment is a useful tool for making large phonetically aligned datasets available with relatively little investment. Forced alignment can be performed on a twenty-minute recording in a matter of minutes, while it could take a human transcriber hours to provide the same information. As more researchers use large spontaneous speech datasets, whether recorded in the lab or collected from other sources, they become more reliant on automatic methods for extracting data from the corpus. For example, if we wanted to analyze the vowel inventory of older speakers in Ohio, we might try using the Buckeye Corpus. As mentioned earlier, this corpus conveniently comes with time-aligned markup files indicating the word and phone boundaries. Human transcribers are inconsistent in how they mark boundaries individually and across transcribers, even when strict rules are provided to them. While this inconsistency can be mitigated with clear instructions and processes for phone-level markup, these will not remove all of the inconsistency. Forced-alignment systems, however, make consistent errors in that the set of rules are consistently applied by the algorithm.

While forced alignment is a useful tool, it is important to be aware of the disadvantages that come with it. For instance, forced-alignment systems struggle with properly aligning overlapping speech (a common feature of spontaneous speech). Also, many alignment systems are restricted to words in the pre-populated dictionary (though new words and pronunciation variants can be added manually). This also limits the alignment to a largely phonemic transcription or at best an allophonic transcription, which can account for some pronunciation variation but can be very limiting if the researcher intends to use the transcription as a source of phonetic variation. Moreover, pronunciation variants can cause additional problems, as the system attempts to align phones that the dictionary says should be there but have been reduced or deleted (as in the reduction examples in the introduction). These deletions can lead to cascading errors where deletion errors offset the system by a phoneme causing subsequent phonemes to be out of alignment (Dall et al., 2016). While it is possible to include most common reduced forms, it is difficult to list all possibilities.

Another disadvantage is that most current forced-alignment systems use a 10-ms frame advance or step size for analyzing speech (e.g., Yuan and Liberman, 2008; McAuliffe et al., 2017; Ochshorn and Sloetjes, 2017). That is, a researcher interested in analyzing the duration of a phone in a corpus should not be surprised when the durations are in 10 ms groupings (as illustrated by the peaks in 10-ms steps in Figure 4), starting at 30 ms as the shortest duration. Figure 4 is a density plot comparing phone durations extracted from three corpora using two different forced-alignment systems: (1) the sociolinguistic interview data from Buckeye Corpus of conversational Speech (Pitt et al., 2007) which used the Entropics Aligner and was subsequently hand-corrected; and (2) 28,000 read words produced by one speaker in the Massive Auditory Lexical Decision stimuli (Tucker et al., 2019a) and spontaneous conversation between friends from the Corpus of Spontaneous Multimodal Interactive Language (CoSMIL: a conversational speech dataset Järvikivi and Tucker, 2015) with both corpora using P2FA (Yuan and Liberman, 2008) for their phonetic alignment. The 10-ms groupings in Figure 4 are the result of the use of a 10-ms step size in the forced-alignment system and 30 ms as the shortest possible duration is based on windowing and aspects of the acoustic model. This result can depend on whether hand-correction has been applied to the alignment. This likely will not have a major impact for certain phonetic measures, but if a researcher is interested in speech sounds with short durations (common in spontaneous speech) or small durational effects, this may reduce the size of an effect or the ability to identify a difference. Please see the following articles for

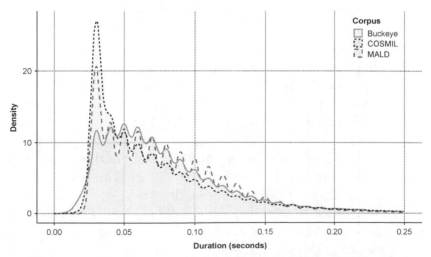

Figure 4 Density plot (using the geom_density() function in the ggplot2 package, Wickham, 2016) of all the segment durations extracted from three different datasets (Buckeye Corpus, MALD, and CoSMIL) using forced-alignment to align individual segments. This figure illustrates that segment durations extracted from these datasets group in intervals of 10-ms.

further discussion of forced-alignment: Bailey (2016); DiCanio et al. (2013); Kominek et al. (2003); Schuppler et al. (2011); Yuan et al. (2018); Dall et al. (2016).

Though we expect the usage of forced-alignment to grow in the field, we would like to note that it should never replace careful manual analysis that involves listening to data (Hawkins, 2003; Coleman, 2003). We believe that this is an important part of understanding the details of the speech, and researchers risk missing important lessons/findings/generalizations about their data when they automate everything and do not manually interact with the data.

Now we turn to the findings in spontaneous speech production research and we start with variability in the signal. While variability is likely dependent on context, we first focus on variability without context and then come back to the role of context.

2.3 Variability in the Signal

Investigation on variability in speech production has attempted to understand the sources of that variability. Researchers have asked: (1) Is the source of variability in speech production inconsistent (i.e., is the variability noise)? (2) Does the speech production system introduce variability for consistent reasons due to cognitive and/or motor system requirements? (3) Is it a combination of consistent and inconsistent variability? If it is a combination, what part of it is consistent and what is inconsistent?

Phonetic corpus research has investigated variability in the speech signal. For example, Ernestus (2000) found many examples of extreme reduction in a Dutch spontaneous speech corpus (e.g., *eigenlijk* produced as /eik/). Work by Johnson (2004) found that over 25 percent of the words in a subset of the Buckeye Corpus are missing phones or segments based on comparisons to the canonical form. In follow-up work, Dilts (2013) investigated the full Buckeye Corpus and found that over 32 percent of the forms in the corpus are different from the dictionary form. Dilts attempted to statistically model the durational variability in the corpus using various frequency-based measures along with linguistic predictors. Work by Greenberg (1999), discussed previously, found massive variability in the four-hour hand-transcribed version of the Switchboard corpus. In addition to the 87 forms of *and*, Greenberg (1999) provides a table of the pronunciation variability of the 100 most common items in the corpus to illustrate how highly variable these productions are, arguing that using the syllable as the basis of analysis might be a fruitful approach in predicting the variability in spontaneous speech.

These variable productions and the seemingly inconsistent way in which they are produced present a challenge for automatic speech recognition systems

(Greenberg, 1999). The variability produced by and across individual speakers increases the difficulty for these systems. Work using spontaneous speech data, like the Switchboard Corpus (Godfrey et al., 1992), investigated ways in which the variation might be accounted for, and as a result, increasing overall recognition accuracy. Bates et al. (2007) use a feature-based system to explore ways to create a better model of pronunciation variation. The feature-based system allows researchers to account for more gradient aspects of phonetic change, as well as prosodic aspects, that contribute to the variability.

Thus far, we have described studies performing phonemic and featural comparisons based on a transcription of the realized form to a dictionary entry or a canonical form. Research on speech variability also makes use of acoustic or articulatory characteristics of production. Acoustic data provides an indirect way to investigate what is happening during speech articulation, and is easier to collect than articulatory data. Duration is the acoustic measure of choice, again likely because of the ease with which it is extracted from a force-aligned speech signal. Cohen Priva and Gleason (2020) have claimed that duration provides a primary insight into the articulatory properties of the speech produced, compared to other acoustic measures for certain speech sounds. However, there are other acoustic measures such as fundamental frequency, formant frequency (the resonant frequencies of the vocal tract which vary depending on the articulatory configuration of the vocal tract, as /i/ and /a/ have different configurations and different resonant frequency patterns), and intensity/amplitude that provide insight into what the articulators are doing. These other measures, in addition to duration, can be used to infer the cognitive and motor processes in speech production. In the remainder of this section, we describe acoustic investigation of speech variability in spontaneous speech.

Research focusing on stops has investigated the acoustic characteristics of the variability in their production (e.g., Lisker and Abramson, 1964; Byrd, 1993; Zue and Laferriere, 1979). A subset of that literature has focused on the variability in spontaneously produced stops across a variety of different languages such as: English (Warner and Tucker, 2011), French (Duez, 1995), Kaqchikel Mayan (Tang and Bennett, 2018), Japanese (Mukai and Tucker, 2017), and German (Kohler, 1990). Raymond et al. (2006) investigated the deletion of word-internal /t, d/ in English. They found that stop deletion is pervasive throughout their data and they argue that word internal stop deletion is the result of two different articulatory processes which depend on the environment in which the alveolar stop occurs. At syllable onset, it is likely due to gradient gestural reduction and in syllable coda position it is likely due to cluster simplification. Warner and Tucker (2011) explored the range of variation in the production of English word-medial stops before an unstressed syllable.

The authors found that the stops are realized variably as stops or approximants; however, in many cases they are not realized at all. They compared speech styles by recording a spontaneous conversation, read paragraphs, and a word list and they found differences between the three speech styles, with increasingly more connected speech styles containing more reductions (stops becoming approximant-like). Warner and Tucker (2011) also found that reduction is common in read speech but they did not find that word frequency (the number of occurrences of a word in a corpus) is predictive of the variability. They argue that inconsistent phonetic variability occurs within the production of the segment as long as the phonological distinction is maintained. They also argue that Keating's window model of coarticulation (Keating, 1990) could be modified to account for the variability in the reduced stops.

It has been claimed that word-medial stops in Japanese also reduce (Maekawa, 2003; Arai, 1999; Arai et al., 2007; Vance, 2008). Arai (1999) reported that the word-medial voiced stop /g/ in the word 大学 'university' /daigakɯ/ is reduced to an approximant as in the word [daiɣakɯ], and in extreme cases, the consonant is completely deleted and the word is realized as [daiakɯ]. Furthermore, the author found that among all occurrences of the phoneme /g/ in the dataset, 20.4 percent of them appear with a clear burst, 72.2 percent of them are realized as [ɣ] without a clear burst, and 7.4 percent of them alternate to [ŋ]. Work by Mukai and Tucker (2017) and Mukai (2020) also investigated the range of acoustic variability in the production of Japanese stops. Mukai (2020) found that the distributional patterns across speech styles for voiced stops are comparable to English (Warner and Tucker, 2011). We suspect that the reason for the similar reduction patterns between English and Japanese is due to language-independent articulatory demands on stop production (Barry and Andreeva, 2001).

In recent unpublished research, we compare the vocalic and consonantal interval duration of read speech to that of spontaneous speech, using rhythm metrics to investigate differences between Japanese and English in their durational variability patterns. Figure 5 shows that read (green) and spontaneous speech (red) have different patterns of variability. The figure contrasts vocalic variation in duration (Varco_V on the y-axis) with consonantal variation in duration (Varco_C on the x-axis, Dellwo, 2006). Both variables represent the coefficient of variation which is the standard deviation of the vowel or consonant duration divided by the mean and multiplied by 100. Thus, higher values represent more variability for vowels or consonants. Spontaneous speech shows a higher degree of variability than read speech in vocalic elements (Varco_V) for English but there is no difference in consonantal elements (Varco_C). In other words, the spontaneous speech has greater variability

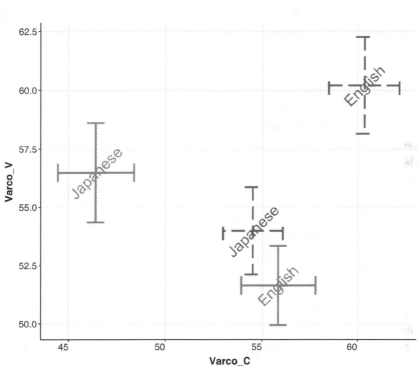

Figure 5 Means of Varco_V (coefficient of variation of vocalic interval duration) and Varco_C (coefficient of variation of consonantal interval duration) in English, and Japanese in spontaneous and read speech. 95% confidence intervals are indicated with lines intersecting at the mean. Labels for the language spoken are centered at the mean.

values than the read speech on the y-axis and both styles of speech demonstrate similar values in consonantal elements on the x-axis. For Japanese, however, spontaneous speech shows a higher degree of variability than the read speech for the consonantal elements (Varco_C) but there is no evidence of a difference between vocalic elements (Varco_V). These findings suggest that spontaneous speech is more variable when compared to read speech, but the way in which this variability is manifested seems to be language-specific. Thus, we see that there is both language-specific and language-independent variation.

Research investigating the vowel system of Yoloxóchitl Mixtec, DiCanio et al. (2015) compared formant measures (vocal tract resonant frequencies) extracted from spontaneous and read speech. The authors found that read speech has a much larger and more distinct vowel space than spontaneous speech. They argued that the difference in vowel space due to style cannot simply be accounted for by decreased vowel duration (i.e., vowel undershoot: the shorter the vowel is, the harder it is for the speaker to achieve an articulatory target Lindblom, 1963). They believe that speakers also make style-specific adjustments to their precision. As a result, they attribute the differences in vowel space to consistent factors related to vowel undershoot, as well as choices about precision in the speakers' production.

Investigation of variability in spontaneous speech has shown that read speech has less variability. We have also shown that this variability is both language dependent and language independent. These results support an approach to speech variability that adopts a combination of both consistent and inconsistent variability.

2.4 Context

It is artificial to discuss speech variability without discussing context. If we take a broad approach to defining context, it includes the environment, the ambient noise, the interlocutor, social factors, and many other possible aspects of conversation. Contextual factors can also be more narrowly focused – like the surrounding phones and words (Bard et al., 1988), phonological neighbor-hood density (Wright, 2004; Munson and Solomon, 2004; Gahl et al., 2012), morphological factors (Plag et al., 2017; Tomaschek et al., 2021a), or word frequency (Wright, 2004; Munson and Solomon, 2004; Linke and Ramscar, 2020). It is likely that the true effect of context is a combination of many or all of these factors, making it difficult to investigate. As discussed earlier, one of the outstanding questions for speech scientists who are interested in spontane-ous speech is the desire to understand the variability in the speech signal and identify where it is consistent or inconsistent. The goal is to identify the con-textual conditions under which variability is realized. These conditions include phonetic, syntactic, semantic, pragmatic, or social factors (van Son et al., 1998). Each condition provides a slightly different explanation or perhaps more pre-cisely, a different perspective on the contributions of context. In the remainder of this section, we describe two of these conditions: predictability and speech rate/prosody.

A number of studies have investigated the role of predictability in spontane-ous speech. These studies seek to quantify the predictability of certain parts of the speech and use this quantification to make predictions about the variability in the speech signal. These studies focus on reduction and use context as a way to identify consistent characteristics of phonetic variability.

For example, using the contextual information surrounding the word of inter-est, researchers have investigated whether the context is predictive of phonetic aspects of that word. This type of work takes the form: "I have X, is it influ-enced by the statistical predictability of the sequence ABX?" Where A and B are some sort of preceding context like phonemes or words and we calculate the predictability of X given that A and B come before X. For instance, they have explored how word duration varies based on the conditional probability of a word (how likely a word is given the surrounding context). In Dutch, van Son et al. (1998) found a consistent relationship between informativity (measured as frequency) and the acoustic characteristics of speech sounds (duration and spectral properties). Specifically, they found that the duration and spectral characteristics are reduced when occurring in highly predictable sequences and enhanced/strengthened in low predictable sequences.

Predictability has been used in order to infer the degree of phonetic or acoustic reduction in a consistent way (Dilts, 2013; Gregory et al., 1999; Bell et al., 2003, 2009; Jurafsky et al., 2001, 2002; Cohen Priva and Gleason, 2020; Cohen, 2014). For example, Dilts (2013) found that word durations are shorter when they occur in a highly predictable context. While much of this research has been limited to Indo-European languages (likely due to the availability of the data), these types of findings have been extended to a few non Indo-European languages. In work on Kaqchikel Mayan (spoken in southern Guatemala), a morphologically complex language, Tang and Bennett (2018) found that contextual predictability influences word duration in content and function words, though the effect is different for the two classes of words. For content words, they found that as preceding context increases in likelihood the duration decreases for content words. For function words, they found that the durations of the words decreased as the likelihood of the following context increases. They also investigated the effect of contextual predictability on the duration of morphemes. However, this effect was not significant. Other research has found that the number of segments in a word and its frequency are predictive of segment deletion in both English and Japanese (Turnbull, 2018). In addition, Turnbull (2018) reported that, while both languages are influenced by predictability, the factors that influence segment deletion vary between languages. For example, higher neighborhood density leads to fewer deletions in English while it leads to more deletions in Japanese. Also, word length, word frequency, and neighborhood density influence the likelihood of deletion in Japanese but not in English. Statistical information about context seems to provide a strong indication that the variability in speech is consistent. However, the results themselves vary depending on the language and other lexical characteristics.

Contextual predictability has also been shown to affect speech variability at the morphological level, more specifically the realization of affixes. Pluymaekers et al. (2005b) found that the frequency of the stem (*eigen* 'own' in *ont-eigenen* 'to disown') influences affix duration (*ont-*) in Dutch – with higher frequency stems predicting shorter affixes. In other research on affixes, Pluymaekers et al. (2005a) found that the number of repetitions and the predictability given by the surrounding words also influence affix duration. Work by Hanique and Ernestus (2011) found that the reduction (durational shortening) and deletion of word-final /t/ in Dutch past participles is predictable from the frequency of the preceding two words. They also found that the frequency of the word relative to its lemma frequency (the total frequency of all forms of a lemma, e.g., jump, jumps, jumped, etc.) is predictive of word-final /t/ reduction. These morphological effects show that many levels of predictability influence the variability in the speech.

Researchers have also found strengthening or enhancement of segments in spontaneous speech as opposed to reduction. Tily and Kuperman (2012) found that the optional Dutch epenthetic schwa (e.g., *melk* 'milk' can be produced as /mɜlk/ or /mɜlək/) tends to be longer for less frequent words. They concluded that speakers are strengthening the acoustic signal to create a more efficient method of transmitting the signal in line with notions of the Smooth Signal Redundancy Hypothesis (Aylett and Turk, 2004). Kuperman et al. (2007) found enhancement of compound interfixes (-*s*- or -*e*(*n*)-) in Dutch. Surprisingly, they found that more probable interfixes are produced with longer duration. This finding does not fit with the predictions of the Smooth Signal Redundancy Hypothesis (Aylett and Turk, 2004) and the vast majority of previous research. As a result they proposed the Paradigmatic Signal Enhancement Hypothesis, claiming that the most likely constituent in a morphological paradigm is produced with a longer duration. Kuperman et al. (2007) predicted that paradigmatic enhancement should occur for irregular verbs in English (as in *know* and *knew*). Specifically, they predict that vowel alternations with strong morphological support between the past and present tense will be acoustically more salient. This prediction was pursued by Sims (2016) who investigated the acoustic characteristics of vowels (formant frequencies and duration) in irregular verbs. Sims (2016) found evidence indicating that aspects of the Smooth Signal Redundancy Hypothesis and the Paradigmatic Signal Enhancement Hypothesis both influence the acoustic characteristics of the vowels in irregular English verbs. Cohen (2014) also found support for both hypotheses using read speech. In addition, articulatory investigation has supported these findings (Tomaschek et al., 2021b).

In further research of the role of morphological function and predictability, Plag et al. (2017) found that the acoustic duration of /s/ and /z/ is dependent on morphological status (morphemic vs. non-morphemic) and function. In a follow-up investigation Tomaschek et al. (2021a) found that morphemic /s/ and /z/ are lengthened when playing a greater role in the discrimination of meaning.

Different aspects of the functional predictability, such as the statistical properties of the morphological environment, played a role in predicting enhancement (a type of phonetic variability).

Prosody provides another type of contextual information with which the variability in spontaneous speech is predicted. Work by Aylett and Turk (2004) explored ways in which prosodic structure and redundancy (as measured by word frequency, the likelihood of three syllables occurring together, and givenness) predict durational variation in spontaneous speech. They found an inverse relationship between language redundancy and duration (the more redundant something is, the shorter its duration), a relationship between prosodic prominence and duration, and that much of the durational variance is accounted for by the redundancy and prosodic prominence measures. As noted previously, Aylett and Turk introduced the Smooth Signal Redundancy Hypothesis. In follow-up work, Aylett and Turk (2006) also investigated formant frequencies using a corpus of read speech (as opposed to spontaneous speech) and found that the realization of F1 and F2 (the first two resonant frequencies of the vocal tract) in the speech supports the predictions of the Smooth Signal Redundancy Hypothesis, specifically formants are more central when they occur in likely environments.

Overall speech rate, measured in words or syllables per minute, varies considerably in spontaneous speech. This variability depends on contextual factors, such as individual speakers, the emotional state of the speakers, the type of speaking situations, and the familiarity of the topics being discussed (Goldman-Eisler, 1968). Speech rate can be decomposed into three types: (1) the production rate or speech rate calculated as the number of production units (e.g., word, syllables or phones) per unit time (e.g., duration of the word or utterance) including pauses; (2) the articulation rate which is calculated as the number of production units (e.g., word, syllables or phones) per unit time (e.g., duration of the word or utterance) excluding pauses (Crystal and House, 1990); and (3) the pause rate calculated as the number of pauses per duration of the utterance.

In spontaneous Japanese, unimportant, predictable words tend to be partially or totally deaccented, meaning that the words are reduced (Fujisaki, 1997). Using spontaneous Barcelona Spanish conversation and a map task, Rao (2009) found that words are more likely to be deaccented if (1) they have fewer syllables, (2) they are verbs or adverbs, (3) they are high frequency words and were recently mentioned in the discourse, and (4) they are in initial or medial phrasal position. Rao argues that words that carry less functional load (i.e., importance) are most likely to be deaccented, which may have a communicative function of deemphasizing the importance within the conversation. The functional load of a word provides a consistent way to predict whether a word will be accented or deaccented.

As we have seen previously, spontaneous speech is often compared to read speech. Hirschberg (2000) compared intonational contours of 395 spontaneous utterances to those of read utterances. They found that utterances, such as declaratives and wh-questions, are more likely to be produced with a form of rising intonation in spontaneous speech than in read speech, possibly providing additional context information (e.g., casualness of speech) to convey the intended message. This indicates that in spontaneous speech, speakers make use of prosody to provide additional context.

Laan (1997) compared the speech rate and prosodic features of spontaneous speech to that of read speech (i.e., median F0, F0 range, F0 declination, and F0 variation). Spontaneous and read speech were recorded in such a way that two male speakers spoke to an interviewer about themselves, and then the same speakers later read a transcription of their spontaneous speech. Laan found that spontaneous speech has lower F0, decreased F0 range, and decreased declination. They also found a slower articulation rate for read speech and they attributed this to the lengthening of phonemes, especially fricatives and nasals. Similar results were found in Dellwo et al. (2015), where the degree of F0 variability is decreased in spontaneous speech when compared to read speech and the articulation rate is slower in read speech. These studies indicate that in spontaneous speech prosodic variability is decreased.

Prosodic boundary markers have also been compared between spontaneous and read speech (Blaauw, 1994). The results indicated that (1) additional pauses, creating a full intonational boundary, occur more in spontaneous than in read speech; (2) phrase-internal boundaries are typically realized without boundary-marking pitch movements in spontaneous speech; and (3) falling boundary tunes are more frequent in read than in spontaneous speech. Howell and Kadi-Hanifi (1991) also compared prosodic properties of spontaneous speech to that of read speech. The authors found that read speech is produced with fewer pauses than spontaneous speech. They also found that read speech is more likely to fragment and coalesce tone unit boundaries than spontaneous speech. Using the German Kiel Corpus for Read and Spontaneous Speech (Kohler, 1996), Trouvain et al. (2001) found that spontaneous speech is produced with a faster articulation rate than read speech and that spontaneous speech contains greater variability. In addition, they found that, although spontaneous speech is faster on average, it contains a high number of slow utterances, possibly due to the large number of very short utterances. We suspect that the increased variability in speech rate is likely due to the speaker using rate as a contextual cue to convey additional information about the speech and to provide additional clarity when necessary.

Studies have investigated how speech rate is used as a contextual cue indicating regional identity. Schwab and Avanzi (2015) compared the articulation rate of spontaneous and read speech in seven regional French variations: Paris and Lyon in France; Tournai and Liège in Belgium; and Geneva, Neuchâtel, and Nyon in Switzerland. They found regional differences in articulation rate and an effect of speaking style, where articulation rate was faster in spontaneous speech than in read speech.

Read and spontaneous speech styles are produced differently. This has been illustrated both at the level of the individual sounds and at the level of prosody. We have also seen that probability calculated in several different ways affects speech production. However, depending on the type of probability, researchers have found both reduction and enhancement in the phonetic signal.

2.5 Disfluencies

Disfluencies, hesitations, pauses, and fillers have long been a focus of phonetic spontaneous speech research. Disfluencies are 'phenomena that interrupt the flow of speech and do not add propositional content to an utterance' (Fox Tree, 1995, p. 709). That is, disfluent speech contains interruptions that break the flow of speech, such as repetitions and/or repairs (e.g., false start), filled or silent pauses (e.g., *err*, *uh*, *um*, etc.), fillers (e.g., *Well...*, *Like...*). Disfluencies are common in everyday spontaneous conversations. Approximately 6 percent of words produced in spontaneous American English, appear to be disfluent (Bortfeld et al., 2001; Fox Tree, 1995). Similarly, a study of French broadcast interviews reported disfluencies at a rate of 8 percent (de Boer, 2000). Corley and Stewart (2008) provides a good introduction and overview of disfluencies in spontaneous speech.

Further, Torreira et al. (2010) found that the spontaneous speech in the Nijmegen Corpus of Casual French contains considerably more filled pauses and hesitations than the journalistic speech in the Evaluation de Systemes de Transcription enrichie d'Emissions Radiophoniques corpus. Moreover, Wieling et al. (2016) used multiple corpora containing multiple types of speech (e.g., spontaneous and pseudo-spontaneous speech) in six Germanic languages: English (American and British), Dutch, German, Norwegian, Danish, and Faroese. They identified consistent crosslinguistic patterns of sociolinguistic variation in the use of 'um' and 'uh'; and they reported that the use of 'um' has increased over time relative to the use of 'uh', with younger speakers using 'um' rather than 'uh' more frequently than older speakers. Wieling et al. also found that this pattern of change is led by women and more educated speakers.

Disfluency research has also been driven by speech technology and the use of disfluencies in automatic speech recognition (e.g., Shriberg, 2001; Gabrea and O'Shaughnessy, 2000). Researchers have sought to understand the functional role of disfluencies in spontaneous speech (e.g., Freeman et al., 2015). It has been claimed that speech errors or filled pauses provide the speaker a moment to think while maintaining their turn in the conversation. It is also possible that disfluencies are a type of marker used as a way to indicate stance (the speaker's attitude) during a conversation (Le Grézause, 2017). Of particular interest for the present overview are the acoustic characteristics of disfluencies. Among other things, there have been investigation of the duration of filled pauses and their component phones (e.g., Lickley, 1994; Shriberg, 2001), the fundamental frequency of filled pauses (e.g., Shriberg, 1994), and the spectral properties of vowels in filled pauses (e.g., Gabrea and O'Shaughnessy, 2000).

The occurrence of disfluencies is not arbitrary or inconsistent. For example, when a speaker is faced with multiple semantic or syntactic possibilities, hesitations are most likely to be observed before low frequency and unpredictable words (Schachter et al., 1991; Levelt, 1983; Schnadt and Corley, 2006). Moreover, disfluency frequency in spontaneous speech is context dependent. For instance, in human-computer dialogue, disfluencies appear at a rate of under 1 percent, but in spontaneous conversation, the rate increases to around five to ten percent (Shriberg, 2001). These distributional differences are likely based on different cognitive demands in speaking tasks (Levelt, 1983). For example, Moniz et al. (2014) indicate that speaking style affects the production of disfluencies in terms of distributional patterns and prosodic properties, where speakers produce more repetitions and fragments, and disfluencies are shorter in dialogues than in lectures. Bell et al. (2003) reported that high-frequency monosyllabic function words are longer or unreduced when preceding or following disfluencies (e.g., filled pauses). They suggest that these results reflect speaker difficulties in utterance planning. Work by Megyesi and Gustafson-Capkova (2002) investigated the relationship between pause patterns, syntactic features, and discourse boundaries in read and spontaneous speech. They asked five listeners to label changes in topic in sentences. They found that in spontaneous speech, the majority of pauses appear at weak boundary positions (labeled as a possible theme shift due to low rater agreement) or at theme continuation points (no change in topic) between or within phrases. For read speech they found that pauses occur in strong discourse boundary positions mainly between sentences.

A number of studies have investigated the relationship between disfluencies and age using spontaneous speech. Taschenberger et al. (2019) found fewer filled pauses as age increased, although only in more adverse speaking conditions. They also found a high degree of individual differences in the use of disfluency adaptations. Other researchers found that while the rate of disfluencies appears to be comparable between younger and older adults in spontaneous narratives (less cognitively demanding), it appears to be greater for younger adults in more cognitively demanding tasks (Bóna, 2011). However, Keszler and Bóna (2019) found no clear connection between age and fluency in terms of pause characteristics and disfluencies in a multi-decade longitudinal study.

While it is common to investigate disfluencies from the desire to understand the human capacity for language, it is important to understand how and why they are produced. Disfluencies are used as a window into understanding human cognition. Disfluencies are also used in speech technology to improve speech synthesis and recognition (e.g., Freeman et al., 2015; Lickley and Bard, 1998).

2.6 Summary

In this section, we described findings which illustrate that there is a tremendous amount of variability in spontaneous speech and that spontaneous speech is acoustically different from read speech. These differences are important, as they allow researchers to better understand the full range of speech phenomena.

Context plays a crucial role for identifying, describing, and understanding the variability in spontaneous speech. Context also contributes to the prediction of variability. There is an abundance of additional context types, beyond what we described, that could and should be considered in future research. Investigation of disfluencies has shown that their realization depends on speech style (read vs. spontaneous speech). Further, it has been shown that disfluencies offer a window into cognitive aspects of speech production.

3 Perception

We now turn to the investigation of perception. In this section, we briefly discuss models, theories, and hypotheses concerned with the perception of spontaneous speech. We then describe methods for conducting perception research with spontaneous speech. This section then includes a description of differences between speech styles, variability, context, and disfluencies. We use the term perception broadly so that it includes perception at the segmental and lexical (spoken word recognition) levels.

3.1 Models and Theories

Since we approach speech perception in a fairly broad fashion, a variety of models, theories, and hypotheses are relevant. In this section, we group them into two: (1) Standard models of speech perception and (2) Models of spoken word recognition. We discuss the components of these models and theories particularly relevant to spontaneous speech research.

Standard models of speech perception can be divided into two categories. The first is motor theories, where in its most basic form, the object of perception is the articulatory gesture (Galantucci et al., 2006, for a review from this perspective). In other words, when a listener perceives speech, they attempt to map the incoming signal to the articulatory speech gestures that would produce them, and these gestures act as an invariant step between the signal and perception. The second category is auditory theories. These theories claim that the object of perception is the acoustic/auditory event (Diehl et al., 2004, for a review from this perspective). There has been a long debate about these two approaches to speech perception and which is correct (e.g., Diehl et al., 2004; Galantucci et al., 2006; Kiefte and Nearey, 2019; Samuel, 2011). There have also been proposals (e.g., Nearey, 1995) claiming that combinations of both approaches are necessary to account for speech perception.

The challenge, from a spontaneous speech perspective, is that none of these models are designed to deal with the additional variability inherent in spontaneous speech (e.g., Mitterer and Ernestus, 2006). In a way, researchers interested in spontaneous speech are introducing additional variability that a listener must be able to deal with, which could be thought of as an extension of the classic 'lack of invariance' problem in speech perception (e.g., Liberman et al., 1967; Appelbaum, 1996). A problem that refers to the fact that there is no simple mapping between the acoustic signal and corresponding linguistic representation. A motor theorist might argue that since the object of perception is a motor gesture, as long as there is just enough information in the signal to cue that gesture, that is all that is necessary for perception. An auditorist might suggest that spontaneous speech still must contain sufficient cues from the speech sound itself, along with the surrounding context to match the auditory input to its phonetic and lexical output. These theories and models of perception focus on the recognition of individual phones and rarely on the recognition of words (cp. Klatt and Klatt, 1990).

Models of spoken word recognition focus on the identification of the 'word'. As in models of speech perception, conceptual and computational spoken word recognition models have not been designed to deal with the variability inherent in spontaneous speech. While we do not go into great detail with regard to the 'ins and outs' of these models, we refer the interested reader to the following articles: (Weber and Scharenborg, 2012; McQueen, 2007; Luce and Pisoni, 1998). One of the issues with these models is the flow of information in the recognition process. In other words, is the flow *top-down* or *bottom-up*?

Bottom-up indicates that the listener does not rely on higher level information for their recognition of words. The basic assumption is that there is enough information in the signal for the listener to recognize a word without higher level information needing to play a role (e.g., Norris and McQueen, 2008). The top-down models, however, allow for information to flow in both directions, so that social, semantic, syntactic, or morphological information (e.g., Niedzielski, 1999; Jannedy et al., 2015) influence the recognition process by modulating expectations about and classification processes of acoustic signals (e.g., McClelland et al., 2006; McQueen et al., 2006).

Another topic that is frequently discussed in models of spoken word recognition is representation. That is, what is the cognitive nature of the words to be recognized (e.g., Marslen-Wilson et al., 1995; Ranbom and Connine, 2007)? From a spontaneous speech perspective, can the variability in the speech signal teach us anything about how words are stored and represented in the mind? One approach to lexical representation is to posit abstractions or prototype representations (e.g., Marslen-Wilson et al., 1995). For example, a listener needs to map the incoming signal to the abstract representation. This entails then that the more variable the signal is from the representation, the harder it will be to recognize. An alternative approach to the representation question is an appeal to exemplar representation (Johnson, 1997; Goldinger, 1996; Hintzman, 1986; Nosofsky, 1990). In this case, the simple view of exemplar models is that listeners store all instances of everything they hear, and a listener classifies the incoming sounds based on their experience. One of the advantages of an exemplar approach is that it provides a way to account for the variability in the signal. The creation of hybrid models followed the early exemplar models, which allow for aspects of both abstract and exemplar approaches to be part of the representational system (e.g., Connine et al., 2008; Cutler and Weber, 2007; Ernestus, 2014; Goldinger, 2007).

These models have long been concerned with the variation in the speech signal and how to deal with it, though the research has largely focused on phonological variability and not phonetic variability. Gaskell (2003) argued for a probabilistic connectionist model which would learn to compensate for articulatory assimilation. This type of connectionist model is an interesting proposal for dealing with assimilatory processes but does not deal with non-assimiltory processes that also occur with reduction (e.g., Mitterer and Ernestus, 2006).

The majority of these models and theories, have not attempted to directly account for spontaneous speech in spoken word recognition or speech perception. Work by Arnold et al. (2017) is the only case of a computational word recognition model that we are aware of that specifically attempts to deal with spontaneous speech and its variability. Arnold et al. used an error-driven learning approach to model speech perception. Subsequent iterations of this model, LDL-Auris (Shafaei-Bajestan et al., 2021), have continued on this theme.

The research, to be described in Sections 3.2–3.6, has attempted to integrate itself into the existing models by proposing changes to the models instead of creating independent hypotheses about spontaneous speech recognition. This is in contrast to speech production, where researchers have developed several hypotheses to account for properties of speech production. As work on spontaneous speech perception progresses, we hope that more specific hypotheses will emerge.

3.2 Research Methods

Investigating perception using spontaneous speech is challenging. This stems from the fact that most of our experimental techniques are designed to work with carefully designed and controlled laboratory speech. Consider the difficulties posed by spontaneous speech. In a conversation between interlocutors with speech freely flowing, there is no simple way to pause the conversation and infer or 'tap into' what is happening at the cognitive level for the listener. While researchers have come up with creative approaches to attacking this question, we are currently not aware of any method that has successfully tapped into the listeners' perceptual processes during conversation. We are, however, hopeful that methods and techniques not yet developed will better allow us to investigate these processes. In the remainder of this subsection, we discuss methods for creating stimuli and tasks that can be used with these stimuli in perception experiments.

We group the stimulus creation into two classes: (1) pseudo-spontaneous speech and (2) spontaneous speech. In both cases, researchers attempt to bring aspects of spontaneous speech into the lab and test perception using relatively standard laboratory techniques. The first approach, pseudo-spontaneous speech, utilizes knowledge gained from studying the production of phones and words in spontaneous speech. They then create controlled or controllable stimuli recorded in a non-spontaneous manner that mirror the characteristics described in the spontaneous production. For example, in word-medial stops it has been shown that English speakers produce a wide range of variation with productions of stops, resulting in deletion, approximation, flapping, durational shortening, and occasionally durational lengthening (Tucker and Warner, 2007; Tucker, 2011, as illustrated in Figure 6). To create the stimuli, the researcher records a speaker and asks them to produce a set of word stimuli multiple times varying the speed and the 'care' with which they are speaking. Speakers are quite good at producing variable stimuli. The researcher then selects stimuli

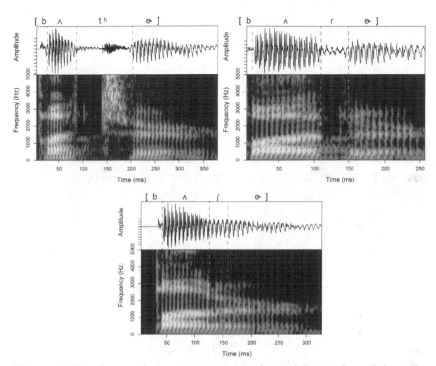

Figure 6 Waveform and spectrogram comparison of the word-medial stop in the word *butter*. Each item includes a transcription of the word above the waveform with dashed lines indicating the approximate boundary for each phone. Top Left: Orthographic pronunciation [bʌtʰɚ] (audio file below) with an aspirated word-medial /t/. Top Right: Flapped pronunciation [bʌɾɚ] (audio file below). Bottom: Approximated word-medial stop [bʌɾɚ] (audio file below).

Sound 2 Audio file available at www.cambridge.org/butter_th

Sound 3 Audio file available at www.cambridge.org/butter_flap

Sound 4 Audio file available at www.cambridge.org/butter_approx

from these laboratory recordings that reflect or most closely approximate the types of realizations found in spontaneous speech.

Using pseudo-spontaneous stimuli is advantageous in the sense that the investigator has a set of stimuli that have been carefully recorded and selected to match the design of the experiment. Most, if not all, experimental tasks are viable options when using pseudo-spontaneous speech. Many studies interested in spontaneous speech have employed this technique (e.g., Sumner and Samuel, 2005; Sumner, 2013; Pitt, 2009; Tucker, 2011; McLennan et al., 2003; Ernestus and Baayen, 2007). The disadvantage is perhaps obvious: the speech is not genuinely spontaneous and at best it is an approximation of spontaneous speech. As a result, listeners might interact with the stimuli differently than they would with genuine spontaneous speech. Investigators sometimes manipulate the acoustic characteristics of the speech, using speech synthesis techniques, to better approximate particular research questions (e.g., Warner et al., 2009).

The second method utilizes spontaneous speech from a corpus or elicited recording of spontaneous speech. For example, the researcher identifies a set of stimuli of interest in a recording, and then extracts the sections of speech. The excised speech samples are then used as stimuli in various experimental tasks (e.g., Arnold et al., 2017; Ernestus et al., 2002; Koch and Janse, 2016; Podlubny et al., 2018; Van de Ven et al., 2012). Excising stimuli from recorded spontaneous speech is an excellent way to create natural experimental stimuli. The difficulty is that the stimuli are removed from their surrounding context which is likely to be important for their recognition (e.g., Ernestus et al., 2002). This approach can also make it difficult to find sufficient stimuli for conditions of interest, and as a result, it limits the research questions that might be asked and the tasks that might be used.

As noted earlier in this section, using pseudo-spontaneous stimuli allows one to use any task that fits one's research question. These include different varieties of discrimination and identification behavioural tasks. A special issue published in *Language and Cognitive Processes* provides a detailed description of many of these tasks in spoken word recognition (Grosjean and Frauenfelder, 1996). As noted previously, when using spontaneous speech, the task options are substantially limited. While many of the same tasks are possible, the task selection is limited to the researchers' ability to generate appropriate stimuli for the task using existing speech. For example, an auditory lexical decision task (a listener is asked to decide if what they hear is a word or a made-up word) would be difficult to conduct because pseudowords are required as part of the task.

Researchers investigating the perception of spontaneous speech would most likely prefer to make use of a fully ecologically valid task. However, it is difficult to design a study that tests perception and also employs spontaneous speech with an ecologically valid task. It may be possible to use brain imaging or pupil dilation methods (more is said about these tasks in Sections 3.4 and 3.6), which could monitor cognitive effort during a conversation. In this case, the researcher would be presented with the challenge of inferring what aspects of the conversational speech is initiating changes in cognitive load. While it might be due to aspects related to the processing of speech, it might also be related to other aspects of the conversation or environment. Because conversational speech progresses so quickly, these methods may be too slow to determine the cause of increases in cognitive load.

3.3 Distinguishing between Speech Styles

Several studies have investigated the contribution of prosodic structures (such as stress and intonation) to the identification of spontaneous versus read speech. For instance, Levin et al. (1982) found that listeners are able to identify the speech style despite the fact that these speech segments are low-pass filtered (high-frequency information is removed from the signal). Batliner et al. (1995) demonstrated that, while a single prosodic feature does not differentiate between spontaneous and read speech, read and spontaneous speech are well distinguished when considering a set of features together. Similar results were found in Laan (1997) where they examined the predictive power of prosodic features for the classification of speech styles and found that F0 declination and articulation rate are predictive for the proportion of spontaneous classifications. However, research by Dellwo et al. (2015) found that prosodic and temporal variability cannot predict the accuracy of the classification of speech style well.

Brouwer et al. (2010) found that participants shadowing sentences from a spontaneous speech corpus produced shorter durations for the reduced items and longer durations for the carefully produced items, indicating that listeners are able to clearly distinguish between the speech styles. However, the difference between the reduced and carefully produced items was much smaller in shadowed productions than in the original. This reduced difference, they found, was due to participants' possible reconstructions of canonical forms from reduced forms.

3.4 Variability Affects Perception

Similar to spontaneous speech production, research on variability in the speech signal is a major subarea in perception. The goal for this area of research is to understand what variability in the signal, also described as fine phonetic detail (e.g., Hawkins, 2003), listeners utilize to understand the message being conveyed. Further, it is important to understand what changes to the signal increase or decrease comprehensibility.

It has been found that reduction inhibits the perception of spontaneous speech (e.g., Ernestus and Baayen, 2007; Tucker, 2007; Van de Ven et al., 2011; Ranbom and Connine, 2007; Brouwer et al., 2012b). For example, Mukai (2020) investigated the perception of Japanese words in isolation with pseudo-spontaneous and read speech as indicated by pupil dilation. Pupillometry is the measurement of pupil dilation and has been utilized as an index of cognitive effort, such that greater dilation indicates greater cognitive effort (for more information on the relationship between pupil dilation and cognitive effort (see Kahneman and Beatty, 1966; Laeng et al., 2012; Papesh and Goldinger, 2015). Mukai found that reduced forms elicit larger dilation than unreduced forms as illustrated by the left side of Figure 7. This result suggests that the reduced productions inhibit speech recognition. Researchers have argued that one of the reasons for this inhibition is that the reduction makes it more difficult for listeners to match the incoming stimulus with their cognitive representation for this word. However, variability due to reduction has also elicited results indicating that reduced speech facilitates recognition (e.g., McLennan et al., 2003; Sumner, 2013; Van de Ven and Ernestus, 2018). These results argue that the form listeners have the most experience with, the spontaneous speech form, should be recognized more quickly than forms that are less common.

On the surface, these inhibition and facilitation findings seem to be contradictory. However, when the results are considered carefully, these conflicting findings likely lie in the way in which reduction is treated by the individual researchers. To illustrate our point, we describe two studies which examined the perception of word-medial stops. McLennan et al. (2003) investigated word-medial /t/ and /d/ with carefully and casually produced stimuli (n.b. McLennan et al. (2003) were not investigating aspects of spontaneous speech specifically but allophonic variation in pronunciation). For McLennan et al., the casual form of their stimuli was a flapped realization of the word-medial /t/ or /d/ (e.g., *atom* [ærəm]) and the careful form was an unflapped version of the same word (e.g., [ætəm]). They found faster responses for flapped stimuli as opposed to unflapped stimuli. In contrast, using pseudo-spontaneous speech, Tucker (2011) found faster responses for unreduced items when compared to

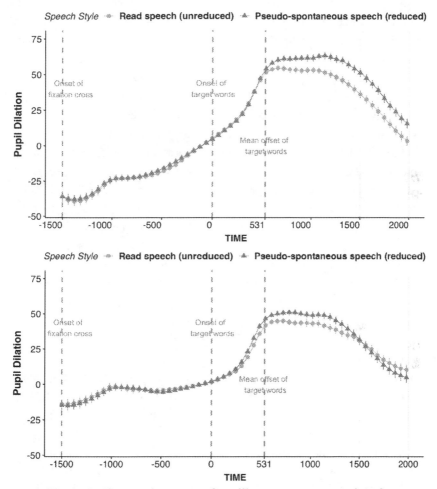

Figure 7 The grand average of pupillary responses over time for pseudo-spontaneous speech (reduced) and read speech (unreduced) forms in L1 (left) and L2 (right) listeners (Mukai, 2020).

reduced items. There is a change in terminology between the studies. In Tucker (2011) an unreduced flap was still a flap [æɾəm], while the reduced flap was shorter and frequently produced as an approximated flap [æɾəm], where the tongue does not create a complete closure during articulation resulting in an approximant (see Figure 6). McLennan et al. (2003), however, compared the flapped realization to an unflapped realization. It would be quite simple to equate casual with reduced and careful with unreduced and conclude that these results are contradictory when in fact they are most likely complementary (as previously observed by Zimmerer and Reetz, 2014). It seems likely that these results represent different parts of a reduction continuum.

As seen on the right-hand side of Figure 7, Mukai (2020) also investigated the differences between native (left) and non-native (right) listeners of Japanese. All listeners showed similar patterns, but native listeners have a greater difference between the pseudo-spontaneous (reduced) and read speech (unreduced) than non-native listeners. In a study of how second language listeners deal with variability due to spontaneous speech, Mitterer and Tuinman (2012) investigated German learners of Dutch and how they produced and perceive word-final /t/ deletion with pseudo-spontaneous speech. In their analysis of the production data, they report that both Dutch and German speakers' word-final /t/ deletion patterned similarly but that when /t/ occurred in a verbal inflection they patterned differently. They found that the unfamiliar spontaneous speech process found in the verbal inflection, which does not occur in their native language, creates challenges for L2 learners of Dutch. It has also been shown that it is more difficult for second language learners to recover variability in casual speech than for native listeners (Tuinman et al., 2012). For researchers interested in second language perception and spontaneous speech, Ernestus et al. (2017a) investigate how reduction impacts advanced language learners and Ernestus et al. (2017b) study the impact of native language phonotactic constraints on the perception of a second language.

Sumner and Samuel (2005) investigated the perception of the allophonic variants of word-final /t/ in English. They found that the variants /t/: [t], [ʔt˺], [ʔ] prime semantically related words equally well with relatively short primes, but when they used a long-term priming technique, they found that [t] is a better prime than the variants. Mitterer and Ernestus (2006) investigated the deletion of word-final /t/ in Dutch. In a series of production and perception studies, the authors found that information from the surrounding phones, such as a short duration /s/, strongly influence the recognition of whether a /t/ is present or not, and when a deleted sound does not result in an additional competitor from a homophonous word that does not have the /t/, listeners are much more likely to respond that the word has a /t/. Zimmerer and Reetz (2014) replicated and extended this study, using German to investigate the perception of word final /t/. These studies indicate that listeners find variant productions more difficult to perceive than the canonical production and that they make use of all available information for perception.

Brouwer et al. (2012b) investigated the role of phonological competition in a sequence of eye-tracking experiments. They found that listeners relax their expectations when reduced speech is present in the experiment. In a related study Brouwer et al. (2012a) found that when listeners hear reduced forms (e.g., [pjutər] for *computer*), they are more likely to be distracted by forms that are phonologically similar (e.g., *pupil*) to the reduced form as opposed to the unreduced form. They showed that reduced forms with and without context have more phonological competition than unreduced forms. Mitterer and McQueen (2009) replicated previous results on /t/ deletion (Mitterer and Ernestus, 2006), using a four-choice written word eye-tracking experiment. Listeners heard pseudo-spontaneous words in sentential context that are ambiguous in Dutch. For example, the casual pronunciation of *kast* 'cupboard' as [kas] which has the final /t/ deleted – causes the word to compete with the word *kas* 'green house'. They found that listeners rely on the predictability of the deletion based on the context when disambiguating between competing forms. Much of the research on variability has also investigated the role of context in the recognition of forms produced in spontaneous speech.

Speech variability in its different forms and at different levels of structure has both inhibitory (e.g., slower responses with more errors) and facilitatory (e.g., faster responses with fewer errors) effects on perception. Models of speech perception and word recognition need to be able to address variability in its different forms and levels of structure.

3.5 Context

The role of context is a core part of research on the perception of spontaneous speech. All speech is realized in context, even in an experiment where participants are listening to words in isolation as the list itself is a type of context that influences the outcome of the experiment (e.g., Balota et al., 2012; Zevin and Balota, 2000). Context includes the environmental context (like the room), the interlocutor (who the speaking partner is), the phonetic context (the surrounding sounds), the syntactic context (structural information), the prosodic context (the intonational information), and the semantic context (related words appearing in similar proximity). All of these types of context play a role in perception, but the importance of these different types of contexts will vary. Listeners employ all the information available to maximize their comprehension. For example, Pollack and Pickett (1964) found that the intelligibility of read connected speech increases with more context. Ernestus et al. (2002) investigated different types of context in spontaneous Dutch. The authors excised utterances containing extreme reductions from the Ernestus Corpus of Spontaneous Dutch (Ernestus, 2000). The highly reduced productions included words like *natuurlijk* 'of course' produced as [tyk]. The authors created three blocks of stimuli for listeners to transcribe orthographically: (1) the word in isolation; (2) the word with phonetic context (the neighboring vowel and intervening consonant); and (3) the word with sentence context. They found that listeners' word identification accuracy increases as more context is made available (50% →

70% → more than 90%). In the following section, we describe different types of context: phonetic, prosodic, speech rate, and syntactic/semantic.

The immediate phonetic context is an important type of context in the perception of spontaneous speech. Bard et al. (1988) found that following context improves recognition of words using a gating task. Using the phoneme-monitoring task, Kemps et al. (2004) investigated listeners' ability to reconstruct suffixes as a result of reduction in Dutch (e.g., *natuurlijk* 'of course' produced as [tyk]). They found that context influences a listeners' ability to identify the missing suffix, and that both phonology and orthography influence listeners' responses. The authors indicate that when the listener heard a reduction that did not match the orthographic form, their knowledge of how a stimulus should be spelled influenced their response. Research by Tomaschek and Tucker (2021) also found that when suffixes are mismatched in English verbs (e.g., by swapping the *-s* with *-ing* on the verb *talk*) it is more difficult for listeners to identify the suffix. In a similar vein, using pseudo-spontaneous speech, Chen and Tucker (2013) found that the fundamental frequency in preceding and following sonorants improves Mandarin listeners' ability to identify lexical tones. Thus, listeners use information in the surrounding context and lexical knowledge (e.g., phonology or fundamental frequency) to identify missing information such as a missing suffix or tone.

Using excised utterances from a corpus of spontaneous speech, Van de Ven et al. (2012) found that acoustic cues in the context aid the listener in the identification of low predictability missing words and that semantic/syntactic information also aids listeners. In a related study, Podlubny et al. (2018) investigated the role of context and the contribution of specific parts of the acoustic signal. In this study, they selected a set of sentences from a recording of a spontaneous conversation containing targets that range from highly reduced to less reduced. Participants first performed a visual Cloze task, which was subsequently used in the analysis to predict the contextual predictability of the target. This was followed by auditory Cloze tasks containing acoustically manipulated target stimuli. They found significant improvement in comparing performance between visual and auditory Cloze tasks. Providing any acoustic information significantly improved listeners' recognition. This study, like the others in this section, indicates that listeners make use of all available cues.

Prosodic information also provides contextual information that listeners use in speech perception. Mehta and Cutler (1988) compared the recognition of spontaneous and read speech using a phoneme-monitoring experiment, in which listeners detected word-initial target phonemes. Results indicated that while overall response times do not differ between the two speech styles, several prosodic features affect the reaction times. In read speech, target phonemes are detected faster when occurring later in a sentence, as well as when they are preceded by longer words. They also found that in spontaneous speech, target phonemes are detected faster in accented words, as well as in strong syllables. McAllister (1991) compared the intelligibility of stressed syllables in spontaneous and read speech. They found that while intelligibility is higher for read speech, intelligibility for spontaneous speech depends on stress, as unstressed syllables are much less intelligible than stressed syllables. Cutler et al. (1997) provide a review of prosody and spoken language recognition with commentary on spontaneous speech.

In two studies, Pollack and Pickett investigated how intelligibility is affected by changes in duration, as a result of the connected nature of the speech (Pickett and Pollack, 1963; Pollack and Pickett, 1963). In Pickett and Pollack (1963), they recorded fluent speech at different rates and then manipulated excised words from the sentences by changing the duration of the utterances to test the effect on intelligibility. They found that (1) shorter durations are less intelligible, and (2) there seems to be an ideal duration, as very long durations also decrease intelligibility. In another study, Pollack and Pickett (1963) excised target words from conversational speech and used these words to test intelligibility. They also found that intelligibility of the speech sounds is directly related to the duration of the speech sounds. Both of these studies indicate that speech rate is an important contextual factor affecting the intelligibility of speech.

More recently, Dellwo et al. (2015) investigated the predictive power of articulation rate for the accuracy of the classification of speech as either spontaneous or read. Results showed that, despite the fact that the articulation rate differs between the two speech styles, it does not predict the accuracy of the classification of speech style well. Koch and Janse (2016) extracted stimuli from the Spoken Dutch Corpus (Oostdijk, 2000) and used eye-tracking to investigate intelligibility. Their results revealed that increased speech rate inhibits recognition and that this effect is equal for both older and younger listeners. Koch and Janse's finding is one of the first studies to investigate older listeners and spontaneous speech. Previous research, not using spontaneous speech, had found that older listeners were less adept at recognizing speech that had been artificially manipulated (e.g., Vaughan et al., 2006). As a result, when speech rate is manipulated naturally, the aging cost disappears.

In an investigation of new (first mention in a monologue) and old (subsequent repetition) words, Fowler and Housum (1987) found that listeners identify old words, presented in isolation, less accurately than new words. They also found that listeners are able to determine if a word is old and new. In an investigation of the role of semantics in perception, Van de Ven et al. (2011) utilized pseudo-spontaneous stimuli in a priming paradigm. The authors suggest that semantic information facilitates the recognition of upcoming words only if there is sufficient processing time to understand the reduced word. Van de Ven et al. (2010) showed that patterns of recognition are similar between native English and late Asian-English bilingual listeners. Additionally, they found that the bilingual listeners show decreased effects of semantics in comparison to the native listeners.

In a similar vein, Brouwer et al. (2013) investigated the recognition of reduced and unreduced (canonical using their terminology) word forms from spontaneous speech. In their experiments they provided the discourse context to the listener to investigate how the listener adapts to the word recognition when the discourse context is made available. In this investigation, the authors asked listeners to rate the strength of the discourse information: weakly supportive and strongly supportive. They found that listeners do not benefit equally from the supportive discourse. In their first experiment, they found that listeners benefit from both types of context. However, they found better identification in the strongly supportive context than the weakly supportive context for reduced forms. In their second experiment they found that listeners benefit equally when provided with unrelated discourse context, allowing the listener to adapt to the speaker.

3.6 Disfluencies

Disfluencies, including hesitations, pauses, fillers, and markers, impact speech perception in spontaneous speech. For instance, Lickley and Bard (1998) investigated listeners' ability to recognize disfluencies in excised spontaneous speech. They found that listeners are not particularly good at identifying disfluencies, but when they do identify one, it is during a word following the break and before word offset. Lickley and Bard (1998) claim that listeners rely on the acoustic signal but not on the semantics or syntax when identifying disfluencies. The fact that listeners find it difficult to identify disfluencies might indicate that they play a functional role in the perception of spontaneous speech.

Furthermore, these disfluencies in spontaneous speech potentially influence listeners in at least two different dimensions in time, namely the moment-to-moment process of determining the speaker's intended meaning and the listener's lasting impression of what was said. Disfluencies have traditionally been treated as 'noise' based on the assumption that they would cause processing issues for listeners (Martin and Strange, 1968). It was thought that these disfluencies had to be excluded to intake the information in the linguistic input (Levelt, 1989). Recent studies, however, suggest that listeners use disfluencies to facilitate comprehension of speech in various ways. For example, research demonstrated that they are used to avoid syntactic parsing errors (Fox Tree, 2001), to speed up word recognition (Corley and Hartsuiker, 2011), to improve recognition memory (Collard et al., 2008), and to facilitate contextually driven predictions for upcoming words (Corley et al., 2007; Mac-Gregor et al., 2009). More specifically, work by Brennan and Schober (2001) found that the disfluency 'uh' cues a shorter upcoming delay, but 'um' signals a longer delay. That is, when listeners detect 'uh' in speech, they heighten attention for upcoming speech; however, they do not do so when 'um' appears as there is no reason for listeners to expect the next upcoming word immediately with 'um'.

3.7 Summary

This section introduced some of the models and theories around perception and how they are relevant to spontaneous speech. The speech used for investigating spontaneous speech was divided into two types: pseudo-spontaneous and spontaneous. The advantages and disadvantages of these different types of stimuli were described. We then discussed how listeners distinguish between different speech styles. Variability in the speech signal with and without context can both inhibit and facilitate perception. It is important to consider how these different effects may complement each other. The final topic discussed in this section was the functional role that disfluency plays in the perception of spontaneous speech.

4 General Summary

In this section, we summarize patterns in the findings and point out common themes. One common finding in production and perception research is that spontaneous speech is different from read and laboratory speech. There are instances where differences are not found, as identical spontaneous and read utterances have more similarities than differences. The motivation for the focus on differences is a matter of perspective. For example, one goal of this type of research is to understand how two utterances conveying the same message are different. In other words: (1) How and why are read and spontaneous speech produced differently? and (2) How do those differences impact perception?

The first question, on the nature of and reasons for differences between read and spontaneous speech, is a common theme for research on spontaneous speech. Many differences have been found, for example, these speech styles have been shown to differ in terms of the segmental and prosodic properties and these differences are perceptually salient to listeners. These differences have been attributed to factors like speech rate, contextual predictability and information load. The second question considers how these differences affect perception. Both inhibitory and facilitatory results have been found when comparing read speech to spontaneous speech and research on this topic has sought to discover why differences occur.

A theme resulting from these comparisons is that care should be taken when comparing across studies. Inhibitory and facilitatory findings seem to contradict each other but the difference may lie in the use of terminology or level of analysis. More investigation is necessary to understand and explain the relationship between these findings.

Context is important in understanding speech variability in both production and perception. When taken out of context, spontaneous utterances are very difficult – if not impossible – to recognize. It is possible to learn useful information about perception and production without context as it simplifies the problem. The type and amount of context also matter, as even a small amount aids the listener's recognition of speech significantly. One demonstration of the effect of context is to present the same reduced utterances in isolation and in context. In many instances the listener will not even notice that there is a reduction when it is produced in context, as is illustrated with the following example. It would be hard to recognize [dætə] to mean *Do you have to* without the context of the full utterance, where the speaker is asking: *Do you have to dial 9 to get out?* (audio file below).

Sound 5 Audio file available at
www.cambridge.org/English_do_you_have_to

For the investigation of spontaneous speech in both production and perception, speech corpora are key resources. Corpora provide a wealth of data and an opportunity to examine many different aspects of spontaneous speech. Further, they provide a resource for stimulus generation.

As a number of studies have pointed out, research on spontaneous speech is important for scholars interested in understanding all aspects of speech communication (Warner, 2011, 2012; Ernestus and Warner, 2011; Tucker and Ernestus, 2016). It is also important that models of speech communication are able to account for processes in laboratory speech and spontaneous speech. For example, models of spoken word recognition have not been designed to deal with effects of extra-lexical context (Subsection 3.5) and struggle to account for the variability in the speech signal (Subsection 3.4). This is not to say that these models cannot account for these aspects of spontaneous speech. In many of the described studies, there have been proposals for modifications to these models that would allow them to account for these phenomena. However, the proposed changes have not been implemented in the models.

Models of speech production also struggle to deal with variability in spontaneous speech. Most cognitive preparation models do not predict beyond the phoneme, which precludes predictions about all aspects of phonetic variability. Motor preparation and execution models, however, have been designed to deal with variability caused by phenomena like gestural overlap. The challenge is that while the motor execution model can produce acoustic output, it does not make predictions about cognitive function. A combined model, similar to Hickok (2014a), could make articulatory or acoustic predictions, based on the cognitive characteristics of the system and these predictions could then be compared to actual patterns in the speech. While this type of work has begun, it has been mostly conceptual.

Investigation of spontaneous speech needs creativity in data creation and experiment design while applying relevant controls to specific questions. Future researchers need to continue creating new methods and techniques in the ongoing investigation of spontaneous speech. We return to this topic in Section 6.

5 Implications: Teaching and Clinical

As we have already mentioned a few implications from the research perspective, we describe implications from the teaching and clinical perspectives in this section. An implication from the teaching perspective is that the nice, neat phonemic inventory that instructors ask introductory linguistics and phonetics students to transcribe is not in fact what is being produced. As has been pointed out by others (Warner and Park, 2018), what speakers actually produce is highly variable and orthographic systems will struggle to reflect that variability. This means that when we teach our students a nice neat phonemic transcription system, we miss an opportunity in helping students understand that the International Phonetic Alphabet (IPA) is, in the end, another orthography that imperfectly represents the acoustic speech signal. While the IPA represents the sounds produced by a speaker much more accurately than a traditional orthographic system (particularly when diacritics are used), this increased accuracy does not mean that the transcription is a perfect reflection of the acoustic signal. Thus, introducing students to spontaneous reduced speech gives them the opportunity to critically think about the uses of the IPA or any transcription system, and instances where it is less useful. The use of spontaneous speech and reductions is also a useful way to engage students in the learning of phonetics (Warner and Park, 2018). Like the examples presented earlier, trying to identify reductions and determine how they were produced is a bit like puzzle solving. It presents an opportunity for students to consider what is going on articulatorily and how those changes might affect the acoustic realization of the reduced sounds.

Investigation of spontaneous speech also leads us to applications that are closely related to daily life, including automatic speech recognition (Speech to Text), speech synthesis (Text to Speech), and second language teaching. For example, the use of technology, such as speech to text and text to speech, has become increasingly widespread. Now we perform many activities on a daily basis involving this technology, such as watching a video online with automatic subtitles, using automatic subtitles during a video conference for those who are hard of hearing, dictating the text of a paper, synthesizing the text of a paper, sending a text message, asking a digital assistant to turn off lights, and scheduling an appointment. As a result, the importance of coping with spontaneous speech in the domain of speech technology has increased, with a focus on conversational speech in language modeling (Zellers et al., 2018).

Teaching and learning a second language is another important area that is intertwined with spontaneous speech. Language learners have experienced confusion when speakers do not pronounce words and sentences the way they were taught in class. Characteristics of spontaneous speech, such as phonetic reduction and deletion, confuse learners when interacting with native speakers in a conversational context. Several studies suggest that it might be helpful to include spontaneous speech in second language teaching so that students recognize the range of pronunciation variants in both production and perception (Warner and Tucker, 2011; Warner, 2011; Shockey, 2008). Only acquiring learner-directed careful speech causes students difficulty understanding natural speech outside the classroom.

Clinicians have long recognized that spontaneous speech is important to their research and clinical practice (e.g., Prins and Bastiaanse, 2004; Lowit et al., 2018; Kempler and Lancker, 2002). For example, treatment performed with patients in the clinic is not helpful if it does not translate to outside of the clinic. A client needs the treatment to impact their speech when they attempt to engage in spontaneous conversation with parents, partners, or caregivers in day-to-day communication. Speech Language Pathologists do tremendous work in assisting their clients to be able to communicate. In many cases, spontaneous conversation is not possible, but for many clients, being able to communicate at all or with greater intelligibility with those around them is their desired outcome. Many of the assessments and treatments for these conditions are lab-based (e.g., reading lists of words or sentences or engaging in predetermined activities; Prins and Bastiaanse, 2004; Lansford and Liss, 2014). This raises the question of what the treatment outcomes are for actual spontaneous conversation and how these impact perception.

One interesting example is hypokinetic dysarthria, where a speaker is unable to produce the full range of motor movements required for speech due to a neuro-degenerative state. This impacts speech in such a way that these speakers become less intelligible. There are amazing treatments that decrease the effects of the disease and have positive outcomes on speech production and intelligibility (e.g., Ahn et al., 2014; Wenke et al., 2010). Two interesting research questions arise from production and perception of hypokinetic dysarthric speech. The first is related to speech production with decreased motor control. That is, how do articulations and the acoustic characteristics of hypokinetic dysarthric speech mirror the types of variation, specifically reductions, found in spontaneous speech, and how do they differ? The second question is how do reductions in spontaneous speech due to hypokinetic dysarthria affect perception? Furthermore, how do treatments, which focus on fairly controlled sets of tasks, translate to everyday communication? And more specifically, do patients benefit more by focusing on more spontaneous tasks? These decisions would depend greatly on the severity and type of the dysarthria. While we have used a type of dysarthria as an example here, these arguments extend to other speech motor disorders across a wide range of patients.

6 New Avenues of Research

As in any field of research, there are new avenues for the investigation of spontaneous speech. One clear take-home message should be that spontaneous speech is an important component of phonetic research. While making this point, we do not seek to discount any other speech style. All speech styles are important to speech science (Wagner et al., 2015) and contribute in different ways to our understanding of speech production and perception.

We also would like to note that it is important that researchers continue engaging with spontaneous speech in as many domains as possible. The investigation of spontaneous speech has entered a very exciting time. New and existing large corpora are becoming increasingly available for languages that have been previously unavailable. Computational systems, such as automatic speech recognition, are making these data more accessible. In addition, Tucker and Ernestus (2016) point out that as new statistical approaches and greater computational power are made available, they can be applied to the analysis of spontaneous speech. As a result, researchers' ability to investigate and understand the nature of spontaneous speech is growing and improving.

We have described literature that compares read vs. spontaneous speech (or a variation of this comparison). It is clear that read speech is different from spontaneous speech in terms of speech rate, prosody, and variability to name a few parameters. In undertaking this comparison researchers, including ourselves, have dichotimized speech styles. We believe that this is likely a choice of convenience, but perhaps it is also a choice, built around providing a clear narrative to the research. As is illustrated in Figure 2 from the introduction, speech and the various speech styles are continuous for many measures. If we believe that speech varies in a continuous way, then we should start to treat the dimensions of speech style in a more continuous way as well. This would involve using measures of variability, like duration, as continuous predictors for various characteristics of interest (e.g., Tucker, 2011).

Along these lines, we believe that reduction is a gradient process and that exploring what it means to be 'reduced' from a gradient perspective is important. Is it possible, then, to quantify the variability in a way that reflects what happens in the signal? And, how meaningful is the variability? For example, if we plotted a hypothetical distribution of the word *and* and identified the peak of this distribution as the most common form, then when we place the various pronunciations of *and* on the distribution, we might find that the pronunciation [ænd] is actually on one of the sides of our distribution. As a result, we might see that the extremes are recognized more slowly (these are the least frequent forms after all). We believe that treating speech variability in this way may explain potentially conflicting findings in the literature around the perception of reduction in spontaneous speech.

In Section 3, we described the use of pseudo-spontaneous speech and spontaneous speech. The use of pseudo-spontaneous speech is a clear limitation and many studies acknowledge this limitation. However, working more with spontaneous speech will also have limitations due to the techniques available, which makes it difficult to perform many types of perception tasks - however it also pushes us to develop new techniques for investigating perception and production of spontaneous speech.

It has also been argued that the time has come for other domains of language research to start to embrace spontaneous 'natural' language (Hamilton and Huth, 2018). One of the main challenges presented to researchers interested in spontaneous speech, particularly in the area of speech perception, is identifying suitable tasks which allow one to engage with the online aspects of perception. We briefly describe two areas where we believe there is great potential. First, pupilometry can be effectively used during the production and perception of spontaneous speech (Zekveld et al., 2010; Winn et al., 2018). There are many challenges in applying this method to spontaneous speech, but it has been shown to be an effective way to measure cognitive effort during listening. Second, techniques such as Functional Near Infrared Spectroscopy may also be useful, as it has the temporal resolution to track the brain activity during a fast moving conversation and it has the ability to measure brain activity with a little more depth than electroencephalography (Bauernfeind et al., 2016).

As has been illustrated and discussed in the context sections, context is an important part of investigating spontaneous speech. The example of *Do you have to* realized as [dætə] is an excellent example of the importance of context. It is very difficult, if not impossible, to recognize [dætə] as *Do you have to* but as soon as the listener hears the following context [dætə daɪl naɪn tə gɛt aʊt] or *Do you have to dial nine to get out?*, the speech is less difficult to recognize. Even speech produced as a list of words or in isolation is produced in context, whether it is the surrounding context of words in a production experiment or it involves a speaker pointing at and exclaiming something. Currently, models of spoken word recognition are limited to the recognition of one word and are not designed to deal with context. Future research in this area needs to allow for context to play a role in the recognition of words and utterances. Importantly, models of production and recognition need to have ways of dealing with the phonetic material that is produced as part of spontaneous speech. Granted, models are meant to be a simplification of the actual system, but if the model is unable to reproduce important aspects of production and recognition (as found in spontaneous speech), these models will always fall short. They will be limited and unable to make predictions about production and perception in spontaneous speech.

One of the areas that we think is important for additional research is the area of individual differences in the production and perception of spontaneous speech. By individual differences we mean how characteristics of an individual speaker or listener influence their production and perception. For instance, there could be an individual difference in the speech production continuum. In this case, one could have two speakers that both produce speech at a similar speech rate in conversation. However, the two speakers may accomplish this speech rate in different ways. For example, speaker A might be a fast and articulate speaker while speaker B makes use of assimilation and deletion strategies to produce speech at this same rate. While this notion of variable individual strategies in the production of spontaneous speech is not new, there is also very little research (that we are aware of) exploring these individual strategies for spontaneous speech production. This type of individual variation could also be reflected in the way that lexical information impacts listeners in perception experiments. Individual speaker variation might also drive listeners to make subconscious choices about how much or how little they need to rely on context for perception.

One area in speech production that we have not mentioned much is speech articulation. While we have not focused much on articulation in this overview, we would like to point out that this is also an important topic and the research on articulation and spontaneous speech is quite limited. While acoustic studies indirectly investigate speech articulation, much more can be learned from investigating the articulation directly. In particular, there are methods such as ultrasound and electromagnetic articulography. A subset of the speakers in the Karl Eberhards Corpus (Arnold and Tomaschek, 2016) were recorded producing spontaneous speech with and without electromagnetic articulagraphy, which should allow for interesting investigations of the articulation and acoustics of spontaneous conversational speech.

The creation of more corpora, along with tools for automatic mark-up, will continue to be a critical tool in spontaneous speech research. It is essential that, as investigation of spontaneous speech progresses, we sample a much larger variety of languages to better understand the crosslinguistic characteristics of spontaneous speech (Tucker and Wright, 2020).

Researchers engaged in language documentation are likely to record spontaneous speech and other communicative events from speakers. The language documentation community has observed that it is important to document a wide variety of communicative events for the purpose of more representative language documentation (Himmelmann, 1998). Documentation of spontaneous speech can take the shape of monologues and stories (rehearsed stories are also collected). While this type of spontaneous speech data is frequently collected, it is less often phonetically analyzed. When this type of data is analyzed, it presents a challenge for typological comparison. This challenge is the result of the lack of comparable data sets for other languages. We hope that future research will allow to make many crosslinguistic comparisons.

Supplementary Reduction Examples

1 Japanese Examples

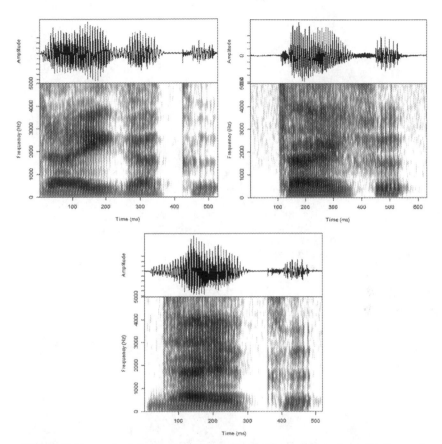

Figure 8 Example from Japanese comparing three different productions of 大学 *Daigaku* 'university'. Top Left: Orthographic production [dɑigɑkɯ]. Top Right: Approximated production [dɑiɣɑkɯ]. Bottom: Deleted production [dɑiɑkɯ].

Sound 6 Audio file available at
www.cambridge.org/Japanese_daiaku_g_dictionaryform

Orthographic production: [dɑigɑkɯ]

Sound 7 Audio file available at
www.cambridge.org/Japanese_daiaku_g_approximated

Approximated production: [dɑiɣɑkɯ]

Sound 8 Audio file available at
www.cambridge.org/Japanese_daiaku_g_deleted

Deleted production: [dɑiɑkɯ]

2 English Examples

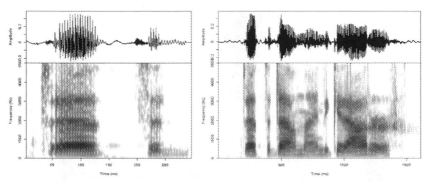

Figure 9 Example from English comparing a sequence of words in isolation
(left) and in context (right): ***Do you have to*** *dial 9 to get out or...?* (that
isolated part is in bold).

Sound 9 Audio file available at
www.cambridge.org/English_do_you_have_to_short

Isolated production

Sound 10 Audio file available at
www.cambridge.org/English_do_you_have_to

Full Context

Below on the top is an example of a statement taken from a spontaneous conversation. On the bottom is the same sequence produced by a different speaker to illustrate what it would look like as carefully produced speech. Both examples are matched for duration.

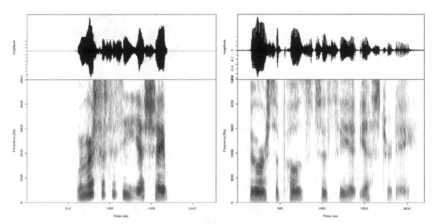

Figure 10 Example from English comparing a spontaneous production (top) and a careful production (bottom) of the sentence: *We were supposed to see it yesterday*.

Sound 11 Audio file available at www.cambridge.org/
English_we_were_supposed_to_see_it_yesterday_silence

Spontaneous production

Sound 12 Audio file available at www.cambridge.org/
English_careful_we_were_supposed_to_see_it_yesterday_silence

Careful production

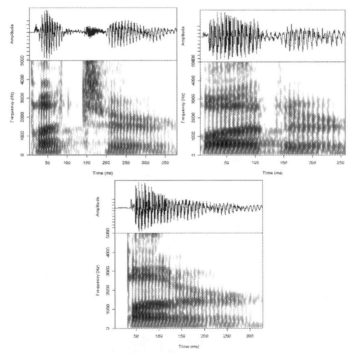

Figure 11 Example from English comparing three different production of
butter. Top Left: Orthographic pronunciation [bʌtʰɚ] with an aspirated
word-medial /t/. Top Right: Flapped pronunciation [bʌɾɚ]. Bottom:
Approximated word-medial stop [bʌɾɚ]

Sound 13 Audio file available at www.cambridge.org/butter_th

Aspirated stop: [bʌtʰɚ]

Sound 14 Audio file available at http://www.cambridge.org/butter_flap

Flapped stop: [bʌɾɚ]

Sound 15 Audio file available at http://www.cambridge.org/butter_approx

Approximated word-medial stop: [bʌɾɚ]

3 Mako Example

Mako examples courtesy of Jorge Rosés Labrada.

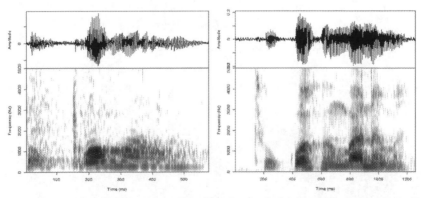

Figure 12 Example of Mako reduction. On the left is the reduced version of /tʰu-kʷ-o hɨbanɨma/ and on the right is slow unreduced version as produced by two different speakers.

tʰu-kʷ-o   hɨbanɨma
3pl-eat-fut   purpose
'(in order for people) to eat' (AB015:8)

Sound 16 Audio file available at http://www.cambridge.org/Mako_reduced

Reduced production

Sound 17 Audio file available at
http://www.cambridge.org/Mako_unreduced

Unreduced production

Rosés Labrada, J. (2015). The Mako language: Vitality, Grammar and Classification. Electronic Thesis and Dissertation Repository. https://ir.lib.uwo.ca/etd/
2851

4 Catalan Example

Catalan examples courtesy of Scott Perry.

The reduced production of *però que hi vols anar?* 'But do you actually want
to go there?' as [pərɔkißɔɫsna] and then produced in an unreduced manner as
[pərɔkeißɔɫzana].

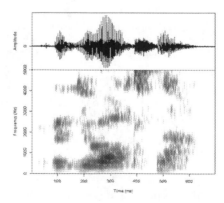

Figure 13 Catalan reduced example: [pərɔkißɔɫsna]

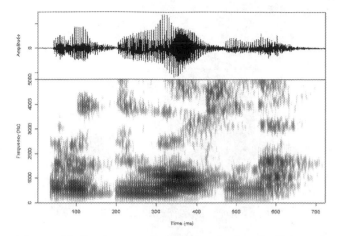

Figure 14 Catalan unreduced example: [pərɔkeißɔɫzana]

Sound 18 Audio file available at
http://www.cambridge.org/Catalan_reduction

Reduced production

Sound 19 Audio file available at
http://www.cambridge.org/Catalan_Unreduced

Unreduced production

5 Estonian Examples

Estonian examples come from the Phonetic Corpus of Estonian Spontaneous Speech.

Lippus, P., Aare, K., Malmi, A., Tuisk, T., & Teras, P. (2021). Phonetic Corpus of Estonian Spontaneous Speech v1.2. https://doi.org/10.23673/re-293

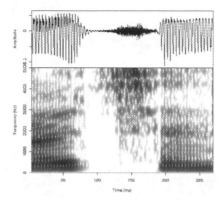

Figure 15 Estonian example: ütlesin [yot:sin]

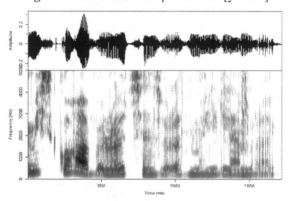

Figure 16 Estonian example: *mis koha peal **ütlesin** sulle et ma hiljem...* 'at which point **did** I **tell** you that I will later...'

Sound 20 Audio file available at
http://www.cambridge.org/Estonian_ekskfk_uumltlesin_5_iso

Utterance in isolation

Sound 21 Audio file available at
http://www.cambridge.org/Estonian_ekskfk_uumltlesin_5_con

Utterance in context

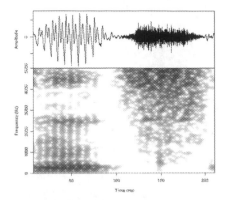

Figure 17 Estonian example: mõttes [mts]

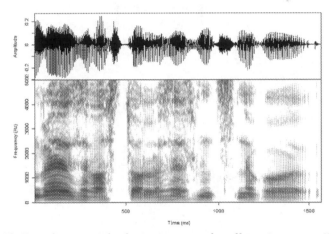

Figure 18 Estonian example: *ka ju see vastuolu selles **mõttes** nagu* "also that is a contraction **in** that **sense** like"

Sound 22 Audio file available at
http://www.cambridge.org/Estonian_ekskfk_motildettes_3_con

Utterance in isolation

Sound 23 Audio file available at
http://www.cambridge.org/Estonian_ekskfk_motildettes_3_con

Utterance in context

6 Spanish Examples

This is an example from the Nijmegen Corpus of Casual Spanish.

Torreira, F., Torreira, F., & Ernestus, M. (2012). Weakening of Intervocalic /s/ in the Nijmegen Corpus of Casual Spanish. *Phonetica*, 69(3), 124–148. https://doi.org/10.1159/000343635

This is an example of *hemos dado* "we have given". If it was produced carefully in could be transcribed as [emos ḏaðo]. However, in the example below it is more like: [emoḏa].

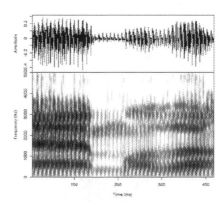

Figure 19 Spanish reduced example in islolation

Sound 24 Audio file available at
http://www.cambridge.org/Spanish_Reduction

Utterance in isolation

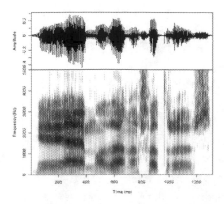

Figure 20 Spanish example in context

Sound 25 Audio file available at
http://www.cambridge.org/Spanish_Full_Context

Utterance in context

References

Ahn, J. S., Van Lancker Sidtis, D., and Sidtis, J. J. (2014). Effects of deep brain stimulation on pausing during spontaneous speech in Parkinson's disease. *Journal of Medical Speech-Language Pathology*, 21(3):179–186.

Alderete, J., Baese-Berk, M., Leung, K., and Goldrick, M. (2021). Cascading activation in phonological planning and articulation: Evidence from spontaneous speech errors. *Cognition*, 210:104577.

Anderson, A. H., Bader, M., Bard, E. G. et al. (1991). The HCRC Map Task Corpus. *Language and Speech*, 34(4):351–366.

Appelbaum, I. (1996). The lack of invariance problem and the goal of speech perception. In *Proceeding of Fourth International Conference on Spoken Language Processing. ICSLP '96*, volume 3, pages 1541–1544.

Arai, T. (1999). A case study of spontaneous speech in Japanese. In *Fourteenth International Congress of Phonetic Sciences*, volume 1, pages 615–618.

Arai, T., Warner, N., and Greenberg, S. (2007). Analysis of spontaneous Japanese in a multi-language telephone-speech corpus. *Acoustical Science and Technology*, 28(1):46–48.

Arnold, D. and Tomaschek, F. (2016). The Karl Eberhards Corpus of spontaneously spoken southern German in dialogues – audio and articulatory recordings. In Draxler, C. and Kleber, F., eds., *Tagungsband der 12: Tagung Phonetik und Phonologie im deutschsprachigen Raum*. Ludwig-Maximilians-Universität München, pages 911.

Arnold, D., Tomaschek, F., Sering, K., Lopez, F., and Baayen, R. H. (2017). Words from spontaneous conversational speech can be recognized with human-like accuracy by an error-driven learning algorithm that discriminates between meanings straight from smart acoustic features, bypassing the phoneme as recognition unit. *PLOS ONE*, 12(4):e0174623.

Aylett, M. and Turk, A. (2004). The Smooth Signal Redundancy Hypothesis: A functional explanation for relationships between redundancy, prosodic prominence, and duration in spontaneous speech. *Language and Speech*, 47(1):31–56.

Aylett, M. and Turk, A. (2006). Language redundancy predicts syllabic duration and the spectral characteristics of vocalic syllable nuclei. *The Journal of the Acoustical Society of America*, 119(5):3048–3058.

Bailey, G. (2016). Automatic detection of sociolinguistic variation using forced alignment. In *Selected Papers from New Ways of Analyzing Variation*, volume 22(2), pages 11–20. https://repository.upenn.edu/pwpl/vol22/iss2/3

Baker, R. and Hazan, V. (2011). DiapixUK: Task materials for the elicitation of multiple spontaneous speech dialogs. *Behavior Research Methods*, 43(3):761–770.

Balota, D. A., Yap, M. J., Hutchison, K. A., and Cortese, M. J. (2012). Megastudies: What do millions (or so) of trials tell us about lexical processing. In J. S. Adelman (Ed.), Visual word recognition: Models and methods, orthography and phonology In *Visual Word Recognition Volume 1: Models and Methods, Orthography and Phonology*, page 90–115. Psychology Press.

Bard, E. G., Shillcock, R. C., and Altmann, G. T. M. (1988). The recognition of words after their acoustic offsets in spontaneous speech: Effects of subsequent context. *Perception & Psychophysics*, 44(5):395–408.

Barry, W. and Andreeva, B. (2001). Cross-language similarities and differences in spontaneous speech patterns. *Journal of the International Phonetic Association*, 31(1):51–66.

Bates, R. A., Ostendorf, M., and Wright, R. A. (2007). Symbolic phonetic features for modeling of pronunciation variation. *Speech Communication*, 49(2):83–97.

Batliner, A., Kompe, R., Kießling, A., Nöth, E., and Niemann, H. (1995). Can you tell apart spontaneous and read speech if you just look at prosody? In Ayuso, A. J. R. and Soler, J. M. L., eds., *Speech Recognition and Coding*, NATO ASI Series, pages 321–324. Springer, Berlin.

Bauernfeind, G., Haumann, S., and Lenarz, T. (2016). fNIRS for future use in auditory diagnostics. *Current Directions in Biomedical Engineering*, 2(1):229–232. Publisher: De Gruyter.

Beckman, M. E. (1997). A typology of spontaneous speech. In Sagisaka, Y., Campbell, N., and Higuchi, N., eds., *Computing Prosody: Computational Models for Processing Spontaneous Speech*, pages 7–26. Springer, New York.

Bell, A., Brenier, J. M., Gregory, M., Girand, C., and Jurafsky, D. (2009). Predictability effects on durations of content and function words in conversational English. *Journal of Memory and Language*, 60(1):92–111.

Bell, A., Jurafsky, D., Fosler-Lussier, E. et al. (2003). Effects of disfluencies, predictability, and utterance position on word form variation in English conversation. *The Journal of the Acoustical Society of America*, 113:1001–1024.

Birkholz, P., Jackel, D., and Kroger, B. (2006). Construction and control of a three-dimensional vocal tract model. In *2006 IEEE International Conference on Acoustics Speed and Signal Processing Proceedings*, volume 1, pages 873–876.

Blaauw, E. (1994). The contribution of prosodic boundary markers to the perceptual difference between read and spontaneous speech. *Speech Communication*, 14(4):359–375.

Bóna, J. (2011). Disfluencies in the spontaneous speech of various age groups: Data from Hungarian. *Govor*, 28(2):95–115. Publisher: Odjel za fonetiku Hrvatskoga filološkoga društva.

Bortfeld, H., Leon, S. D., Bloom, J. E., Schober, M. F., and Brennan, S. E. (2001). Disfluency rates in conversation: Effects of age, relationship, topic, role, and gender. *Language and Speech*, 44(2):123–147.

Bradlow, A. R. and Bent, T. (2002). The clear speech effect for non-native listeners. *The Journal of the Acoustical Society of America*, 112(1):272–284. Publisher: Acoustical Society of America.

Braunwald, S. R. and Brislin, R. W. (1979). The diary method updated. In Ochs, E. and Schieffelin, B. B., eds., *Developmental Pragmatics*, pages 21–42. Academic Press, New York.

Brennan, S. E. and Schober, M. F. (2001). How listeners compensate for disfluencies in spontaneous speech. *Journal of Memory and Language*, 44(2):274–296.

Brouwer, S., Mitterer, H., and Huettig, F. (2010). Shadowing reduced speech and alignment. *The Journal of the Acoustical Society of America*, 128(1):EL32–EL37. Publisher: Acoustical Society of America.

Brouwer, S., Mitterer, H., and Huettig, F. (2012a). Can hearing puter activate pupil? Phonological competition and the processing of reduced spoken words in spontaneous conversations. *Quarterly Journal of Experimental Psychology*, 65(11):2193–2220. Publisher: Sage.

Brouwer, S., Mitterer, H., and Huettig, F. (2012b). Speech reductions change the dynamics of competition during spoken word recognition. *Language and Cognitive Processes*, 27(4):539–571. Publisher: Routledge. https://doi.org/10.1080/01690965.2011.555268.

Brouwer, S., Mitterer, H., and Huettig, F. (2013). Discourse context and the recognition of reduced and canonical spoken words. *Applied Psycholinguistics*, 34(3):519–539. Publisher: Cambridge University Press.

Browman, C. P. and Goldstein, L. (1992). Articulatory phonology: An overview. *Phonetica*, 49(3–4):155–180.

Brown, G., Anderson, A., Shillcock, R., and Yule, G. (1985). *Teaching Talk: Strategies for Production and Assessment*. Cambridge: Cambridge University Press.

Byrd, D. (1993). 54,000 American stops. *UCLA Working Papers in Phonetics*, 83:97–116.

Cangemi, F. and Niebuhr, O. (2018). Rethinking reduction and canonical forms. In Cangemi, F., Clayards, M., Niebuhr, O., Schuppler, B., and Zellers, M., eds., *Rethinking Reduction*, pages 277–302. Berlin, Boston: De Gruyter Mouton.

Chen, T.-Y. and Tucker, B. V. (2013). Sonorant onset pitch as a perceptual cue of lexical tones in Mandarin. *Phonetica*, 70(3):207–239.

Clifton, C., Meyer, A. S., Wurm, L. H., and Treiman, R. (2013). Language comprehension and production. In Healy, A. F., and R. W. Proctor, R. W., eds., *Handbook of Psychology*, 2nd ed. American Cancer Society, pages 523–547. Hoboken: Wiley.

Cohen, C. (2014). Probabilistic reduction and probabilistic enhancement. *Morphology*, 24(4):291–323.

Cohen, C. (2015). Context and paradigms: Two patterns of probabilistic pronunciation variation in Russian agreement suffixes. *The Mental Lexicon*, 10(3):313–338.

Cohen Priva, U. and Gleason, E. (2020). The causal structure of lenition: A case for the causal precedence of durational shortening. *Language*, 96(2):413–448. Publisher: Linguistic Society of America.

Cohen Priva, U. and Jaeger, T. F. (2018). The interdependence of frequency, predictability, and informativity in the segmental domain. *Linguistics Vanguard*, 4(s2). Publisher: De Gruyter Section: Linguistics Vanguard. https://doi-org.login.ezproxy.library.ualberta.ca/10.1515/lingvan-2017-0028

Coleman, J. (2003). Discovering the acoustic correlates of phonological contrasts. *Journal of Phonetics*, 31(3):351–372.

Collard, P., Corley, M., MacGregor, L. J., and Donaldson, D. I. (2008). Attention orienting effects of hesitations in speech: Evidence from ERPs. *Journal of Experimental Psychology: Learning, Memory, and Cognition*, 34(3):696–702. Publisher: American Psychological Association.

Connine, C. M., Ranbom, L. J., and Patterson, D. J. (2008). Processing variant forms in spoken word recognition: The role of variant frequency. *Perception & Psychophysics*, 70(3):403–411.

Corley, M. and Hartsuiker, R. J. (2011). Why *um* helps auditory word recognition: The temporal delay hypothesis. *PLOS ONE*, 6(5):e19792. Publisher: Public Library of Science.

Corley, M., MacGregor, L. J., and Donaldson, D. I. (2007). It's the way that you, er, say it: Hesitations in speech affect language comprehension. *Cognition*, 105(3):658–668.

Corley, M. and Stewart, O. W. (2008). Hesitation Disfluencies in Spontaneous Speech: The Meaning of um. *Language and Linguistics Compass*, 2(4):589–602. _eprint: https://onlinelibrary.wiley.com/doi/pdf/10.1111/j.1749-818X.2008.00068.x.

Coupland, N. (2007). *Style: Language Variation and Identity*. Cambridge University Press. Google-Books-ID: oJE462b0kv4C.

Crystal, T. H. and House, A. S. (1990). Articulation rate and the duration of syllables and stress groups in connected speech. *The Journal of the Acoustical Society of America*, 88(1):101–112. Publisher: Acoustical Society of America.

Cutler, A. (1998). The Recognition of Spoken Words with Variable Representations. In *Proceedings of ESCA workshop on sound patterns of spontaneous speech*, pages 83–92.

Cutler, A., Dahan, D., and van Donselaar, W. (1997). Prosody in the Comprehension of Spoken Language: A Literature Review. *Language and Speech*, 40(2):141–201.

Cutler, A. and Weber, A. (2007). Listening Experience and the Phonetic-to-Lexical Mapping in L2. *ICPhS XVI*, page 6.

Dall, R., Brognaux, S., Richmond, K., Valentini-Botinhao, C., Henter, G. E., Hirschberg, J., Yamagishi, J., and King, S. (2016). Testing the consistency assumption: Pronunciation variant forced alignment in read and spontaneous speech synthesis. In *2016 IEEE International Conference on Acoustics, Speech and Signal Processing (ICASSP)*, pages 5155–5159. ISSN: 2379-190X.

de Boer, B. (2000). Emergence of vowel systems through self-organisation. *AI communications*, 13:27–39.

Dell, G. S., Chang, F., and Griffin, Z. M. (1999). Connectionist Models of Language Production: Lexical Access and Grammatical Encoding. *Cognitive Science*, 23:517–542.

Dellwo, V. (2006). Rhythm and Speech Rate: A Variation Coefficient for deltaC. In Karnowski, P. and Szigeti, I., editors, *Language and language-processing*, pages 231–241. Peter Lang, Frankfurt/Main.

Dellwo, V., Leemann, A., and Kolly, M.-J. (2015). The recognition of read and spontaneous speech in local vernacular: The case of Zurich German. *Journal of Phonetics*, 48:13–28.

DiCanio, C., Nam, H., Amith, J. D., García, R. C., and Whalen, D. H. (2015). Vowel variability in elicited versus spontaneous speech: Evidence from Mixtec. *Journal of Phonetics*, 48:45–59.

DiCanio, C., Nam, H., Whalen, D. H., Timothy Bunnell, H., Amith, J. D., and García, R. C. (2013). Using automatic alignment to analyze endangered language data: Testing the viability of untrained alignment. *The Journal of the Acoustical Society of America*, 134(3):2235–2246.

Diehl, R. L., Lotto, A. J., and Holt, L. L. (2004). Speech Perception. *Annual Review of Psychology*, 55(1):149–179. Publisher: Annual Reviews.

Dilts, P. C. (2013). *Modelling phonetic reduction in a corpus of spoken English using Random Forests and Mixed-Effects Regression*. Thesis, University of Alberta.

Duez, D. (1995). On spontaneous French speech: aspects of the reduction and contextual assimilation of voiced stops. *Journal of Phonetics*, 23(4):407–427.

Ernestus, M. (2000). *Voice assimilation and segment reduction in casual Dutch. A corpus-based study of the phonology-phonetics interface*. LOT, Utrecht.

Ernestus, M. (2014). Acoustic reduction and the roles of abstractions and exemplars in speech processing. *Lingua*, 142:27–41.

Ernestus, M., Baayen, H., and Schreuder, R. (2002). The Recognition of Reduced Word Forms. *Brain and Language*, 81(1):162–173.

Ernestus, M. and Baayen, R. H. (2007). The comprehension of acoustically reduced morphologically complex words: The roles of deletion, duration, and frequency of occurrence. *Proceedings of the 16th International Congress of Phonetic Sciences*, pages 773–776.

Ernestus, M., Dikmans, M. E., and Giezenaar, G. (2017a). Advanced second language learners experience difficulties processing reduced word pronunciation variants. *Dutch Journal of Applied Linguistics*, 6(1):1–20. Publisher: John Benjamins.

Ernestus, M., Kouwenhoven, H., and van Mulken, M. (2017b). The direct and indirect effects of the phonotactic constraints in the listener's native language on the comprehension of reduced and unreduced word pronunciation variants in a foreign language. *Journal of Phonetics*, 62:50–64.

Ernestus, M. and Warner, N. (2011). An introduction to reduced pronunciation variants. *Journal of Phonetics*, 39(SI):253–260.

Ferguson, S. H. and Kewley-Port, D. (2007). Talker Differences in Clear and Conversational Speech: Acoustic Characteristics of Vowels. *Journal of Speech, Language, and Hearing Research*, 50(5):1241–1255. Publisher: American Speech-Language-Hearing Association.

Fowler, C. A. and Housum, J. (1987). Talkers' signaling of "new" and "old" words in speech and listeners' perception and use of the distinction. *Journal of Memory and Language*, 26(5):489–504.

Fox Tree, J. E. (1995). The Effects of False Starts and Repetitions on the Processing of Subsequent Words in Spontaneous Speech. *Journal of Memory and Language*, 34(6):709–738.

Fox Tree, J. E. (2001). Listeners' uses of um and uh in speech comprehension. *Memory & Cognition*, 29(2):320–326.

Freeman, V., Levow, G.-A., Wright, R., and Ostendorf, M. (2015). Investigating the Role of 'yeah' in Stance-Dense Conversation. *INTERSPEECH 2015*, pages 3076–3080.

Frisch, S. A. and Wright, R. (2002). The phonetics of phonological speech errors: An acoustic analysis of slips of the tongue. *Journal of Phonetics*, 30(2):139–162.

Fromkin, V., editor (1984). *Speech Errors as Linguistic Evidence*. Number 77 in Janua Linguarum. De Gruyter Mouton. Publication Title: Speech Errors as Linguistic Evidence.

Fromkin, V. A. (1971). The Non-Anomalous Nature of Anomalous Utterances. *Language*, 47(1):27–52. Publisher: Linguistic Society of America.

Fuchs, R. and Maxwell, O. (2016). The effects of mp3 compression on acoustic measurements of fundamental frequency and pitch range. In *Speech Prosody 2016*. ISCA. ISSN: 2333-2042.

Fujisaki, H. (1997). Prosody, Models, and Spontaneous Speech. In Sagisaka, Y., Campbell, N., and Higuchi, N., editors, *Computing Prosody: Computational Models for Processing Spontaneous Speech*, pages 27–42. Springer US, New York, NY.

Gabrea, M. and O'Shaughnessy, D. (2000). Detection of filled pauses in conversational speech. In *ICSLP 2000*, page 4, Beijing, China.

Gahl, S., Yao, Y., and Johnson, K. (2012). Why reduce? Phonological neighborhood density and phonetic reduction in spontaneous speech. *Journal of Memory and Language*, 66(4):789–806.

Galantucci, B., Fowler, C. A., and Turvey, M. T. (2006). The motor theory of speech perception reviewed. *Psychonomic Bulletin & Review*, 13(3):361–377.

Garrett, M. F. (1975). The analysis of sentence production. In Bower, G. H., editor, *The psychology of learning and motivation*, pages 133–178. Academic Press, New York.

Gaskell, M. G. (2003). Modelling regressive and progressive effects of assimilation in speech perception. *Journal of Phonetics*, 31(3-4):447–463.

Godfrey, J. J., Holliman, E. C., and McDaniel, J. (1992). SWITCHBOARD: telephone speech corpus for research and development. In *[Proceedings] ICASSP-92: 1992 IEEE International Conference on Acoustics, Speech, and Signal Processing*, volume 1, pages 517–520 vol.1. ISSN: 1520-6149.

Goldinger, S. D. (1996). Words and voices: Episodic traces in spoken word identification and recognition memory. *Journal of Experimental Psychology: Learning, Memory, and Cognition*, 22(5):1166–1183. Place: US Publisher: American Psychological Association.

Goldinger, S. D. (2007). A Complementary-Systems Approach to Abstract and Episodic Speech Perception. *ICPhS XVI*, page 6.

Goldman-Eisler, F. (1968). *Psycholinguistics: Experiments in Spontaneous Speech*. Academic P. Google-Books-ID: BAsNAAAAIAAJ.

Gonzalez, J., Cervera, T., and Llau, M. J. (2003). Acoustic Analysis of Pathological Voices Compressedwith MPEG System. *Journal of Voice*, 17(2):126–139.

Greenberg, S. (1999). Speaking in shorthand – A syllable-centric perspective for understanding pronunciation variation. *Speech Communication*, 29(2):159–176.

Greenberg, S., Hollenback, J., and Ellis, D. (1996). Insights into spoken language gleaned from phonetic transcription of the Switchboard corpus. In *International Conference on Spoken Language Processing*.

Gregory, M. L., Raymond, W. D., Bell, A., Fosler-Lussier, E., and Jurafsky, D. (1999). The effects of collocational strength and contextual predictability in lexical production. In *Chicago Linguistic Society*, volume 35, pages 151–166.

Grosjean, F. and Frauenfelder, U. H. (1996). A Guide to Spoken Word Recognition Paradigms: Introduction. *Language and Cognitive Processes*, 11(6):553–558.

Guenther, F. H. (2016). *Neural Control of Speech*. MIT Press. Google-Books-ID: aRSvDAAAQBAJ.

Hamilton, L. S. and Huth, A. G. (2018). The revolution will not be controlled: natural stimuli in speech neuroscience. *Language, Cognition and Neuroscience*, 35(5):573–582.

Hanique, I. and Ernestus, M. (2011). Final /t/ Reduction in Dutch Past-Participles: The Role of Word Predictability and Morphological Decomposability. *INTERSPEECH 2011*, pages 2849–2852.

Hannun, A., Case, C., Casper, J., Catanzaro, B., Diamos, G., Elsen, E., Prenger, R., Satheesh, S., Sengupta, S., Coates, A., and Ng, A. Y. (2014). Deep Speech: Scaling up end-to-end speech recognition. *arXiv:1412.5567 [cs]*. arXiv: 1412.5567.

Harley, T. A. (2013). *The Psychology of Language: From Data to Theory*. Psychology Press. Google-Books-ID: Ax5iAgAAQBAJ.

Hawkins, S. (2003). Roles and representations of systematic fine phonetic detail in speech understanding. *Journal of Phonetics*, 31(3):373–405.

Hickok, G. (2014a). The architecture of speech production and the role of the phoneme in speech processing. *Language, Cognition and Neuroscience*, 29(1):2–20.

Hickok, G. (2014b). Towards an integrated psycholinguistic, neurolinguistic, sensorimotor framework for speech production. *Language, Cognition and Neuroscience*, 29(1):52–59.

Himmelmann, N. P. (1998). Documentary and descriptive linguistics. *Linguistics*, 36(1):161–195. Publisher: Walter de Gruyter, Berlin / New York Section: Linguistics.

Hintzman, D. L. (1986). 'Schema extraction' in a multiple-trace memory model. *Psychological Review*, 95:528–551.

Hirschberg, J. (2000). A Corpus-Based Approach to the Study of Speaking Style. In Horne, M., editor, *Prosody: Theory and Experiment*, volume 14, pages 335–350. Springer Netherlands, Dordrecht. Series Title: Text, Speech and Language Technology.

Howell, P. and Kadi-Hanifi, K. (1991). Comparison of prosodic properties between read and spontaneous speech material. *Speech Communication*, 10(2):163–169.

Hymes, D. H. (1962). On Studying the History of Anthropology. *Kroeber Anthropological Society Papers*, 26:81–86.

Jaeger, T. F. and Buz, E. (2017). Signal Reduction and Linguistic Encoding. In *The Handbook of Psycholinguistics*, pages 38–81. John Wiley & Sons, Ltd.

Jannedy, S., Weirich, M., and Helmeke, L. (2015). Acoustic analyses of differences in [ç] and [\textipa{S}] productions in Hood German. In *Proceedings of the 18th International Congress of Phonetic Sciences*, Glasgow, Scotland.

Jannetts, S., Schaeffler, F., Beck, J., and Cowen, S. (2019). Assessing voice health using smartphones: bias and random error of acoustic voice parameters captured by different smartphone types. *International Journal of Language & Communication Disorders*, 54(2):292–305. _eprint: https://onlinelibrary.wiley.com/doi/pdf/10.1111/1460-6984.12457.

Johnson, K. (1997). The auditory/perceptual basis for speech segmentation. *Ohio State University Working Papers in Linguistics*, 50:101–113.

Johnson, K. (2004). Massive reduction in conversational American English. In *Spontaneous speech: data and analysis. Proceedings of the 1st session of the 10th international symposium*, pages 29–54, Tokyo, Japan.

Järvikivi, J. and Tucker, B. V. (2015). Corpus of Spontaneous Multimodal Interactive Language (CoSMIL).

Jurafsky, D., Bell, A., Gregory, M., and Raymond, W. (2001). Probabilistic relations between words: Evidence from reduction in lexical production. In

Bybee, J. and Hopper, P., editors, *Frequency and the emergence of linguistic structure*, pages 229–254. John Benjamins, Amsterdam.

Jurafsky, D., Bell, A., and Gyrand, C. (2002). The Role of the Lemma in Form Variation. In Gussenhoven, C. and Warner, N., editors, *Papers in Laboratory Phonology VII*, pages 1–34. Mouton de Gruyter, Berlin/New York.

Kahneman, D. and Beatty, J. (1966). Pupil Diameter and Load on Memory. *Science*, 154(3756):1583–1585. Publisher: American Association for the Advancement of Science Section: Reports.

Keating, P. A. (1990). The window model of coarticulation: articulatory evidence. In Kingston, J. and Beckman, M. E., editors, *Papers in Laboratory Phonology: Volume 1: Between the Grammar and Physics of Speech*, volume 1 of *Papers in Laboratory Phonology*, pages 451–470. Cambridge University Press, Cambridge.

Kempler, D. and Lancker, D. V. (2002). Effect of Speech Task on Intelligibility in Dysarthria: A Case Study of Parkinson's Disease. *Brain and Language*, 80(3):449–464.

Kemps, R., Ernestus, M., Schreuder, R., and Baayen, H. (2004). Processing reduced word forms: The suffix restoration effect. *Brain and Language*, 90(1):117–127.

Kendall, T. and Fridland, V. (2021). Sociophonetics, Style and Identity. In *Sociophonetics*, Key Topics in Sociolinguistics, pages 126–155. Cambridge University Press, Cambridge.

Keszler, B. and Bóna, J. (2019). Pausing and disfluencies in elderly speech: Longitudinal case studies. In Rose, R. L. and Eklund, R., editors, *Proceedings of DiSS 2019*, pages 67–70, Budapest, Hungary. ELTE Faculty of Humanities.

Keune, K., Ernestus, M., Hout, R. v., and Baayen, R. H. (2005). Variation in Dutch: From written MOGELIJK to spoken MOK. *Corpus Linguistics and Linguistic Theory*, 1(2):183–223. Publisher: Walter de Gruyter Section: Corpus Linguistics and Linguistic Theory.

Kiefte, M. and Nearey, T. M. (2019). Theories and models of speech perception. In Katz, W. F. and Assmann, P. F., editors, *The Routledge Handbook of Phonetics*, pages 289–313. Routledge. Pages: 289-313 Publication Title: The Routledge Handbook of Phonetics.

Klatt, D. H. and Klatt, L. C. (1990). Analysis, synthesis, and perception of voice quality variations among female and male talkers. *Journal of the Acoustical Society of America*, 87:820–857.

Koch, X. and Janse, E. (2016). Speech rate effects on the processing of conversational speech across the adult life span. *The Journal of the Acoustical Society of America*, 139(4):1618–1636.

Kohler, K. (1996). Labelled data bank of spoken standard German: the Kiel corpus of read/spontaneous speech. In *Proceeding of Fourth International Conference on Spoken Language Processing. ICSLP '96*, volume 3, pages 1938–1941 vol.3.

Kohler, K. J. (1990). Segmental reduction in connected speech in German: phonological effects and phonetic explanations. In Hardcastle, W. J. and Marchal, A., editors, *Speech production and speech modelling*, pages 21–33. Kluwer, Dordrecht.

Kohler, K. J., Peters, B., and Scheffers, M. (2018). *The Kiel Corpus of spoken German: Read and spontaneous speech.*

Kominek, J., Bennett, C. L., and Black, A. W. (2003). Evaluating and Correcting Phoneme Segmentation for Unit Selection Synthesis. In *Eurospeech 2003*, pages 313–316, Geneva.

Kuperman, V., Pluymaekers, M., Ernestus, M., and Baayen, H. (2007). Morphological predictability and acoustic duration of interfixes in Dutch compounds. *The Journal of the Acoustical Society of America*, 121(4):2261–2271.

Laan, G. P. M. (1997). The contribution of intonation, segmental durations, and spectral features to the perception of a spontaneous and a read speaking style. *Speech Communication*, 22(1):43–65.

Labov, W. (1972). *Sociolinguistic Patterns*. University of Pennsylvania Press. Google-Books-ID: hD0PNMu8CfQC.

Laeng, B., Sirois, S., and Gredebäck, G. (2012). Pupillometry: A Window to the Preconscious? *Perspectives on Psychological Science*, 7(1):18–27. Publisher: SAGE Publications Inc.

Lansford, K. L. and Liss, J. M. (2014). Vowel Acoustics in Dysarthria: Mapping to Perception. *Journal of Speech, Language, and Hearing Research*, 57(1):68–80. Publisher: American Speech-Language-Hearing Association.

Le Grézause, E. (2017). *Um and Uh, and the Expression of Stance in Conversational Speech*. PhD thesis, University of Washington.

Levelt, W. J. M. (1983). Monitoring and self-repair in speech. *Cognition*, 14(1):41–104.

Levelt, W. J. M. (1989). *Speaking. From intention to articulation*. The MIT Press, Cambridge, Mass.

Levelt, W. J. M. (1999). Models of word production. *Trends in Cognitive Sciences*, 3(6):223–232.

Levin, H., Schaffer, C. A., and Snow, C. (1982). The Prosodic and Paralinguistic Features of Reading and Telling Stories. *Language and Speech*, 25(1):43–54.

Liberman, A. M., Cooper, F. S., Shankweiler, D. P., and Studdert-Kennedy, M. (1967). Perception of the speech code. *Psychological Review*, 74(6):431–461. Place: US Publisher: American Psychological Association.

Lickley, R. J. (1994). *Detecting disfluency in spontaneous speech*. PhD Thesis, University of Edinburgh, Edinburgh. Accepted: 2017-04-20T10:46:43Z Publisher: The University of Edinburgh.

Lickley, R. J. and Bard, E. G. (1998). When Can Listeners Detect Disfluency in Spontaneous Speech? *Language and Speech*, 41(2):203–226.

Lindblom, B. (1963). Spectrographic Study of Vowel Reduction. *The Journal of the Acoustical Society of America*, 35(11):1773–1781.

Lindblom, B. (1990). Explaining phonetic variation: A sketch of the H&H theory. In Hardcastle, W. J. and Marchal, A., editors, *Speech production and speech modeling*, pages 403–440. Kluwer, Dordrecht.

Linke, M. and Ramscar, M. (2020). How the Probabilistic Structure of Grammatical Context Shapes Speech. *Entropy*, 22(1):90. Number: 1 Publisher: Multidisciplinary Digital Publishing Institute.

Lisker, L. and Abramson, A. S. (1964). A cross-language study of voicing in initial stops: acoustical measurements. *Word*, 20(3):384–422.

Local, J. K., Kelly, J., and Wells, W. H. G. (1986). Towards a phonology of conversation: turn-taking in Tyneside English 1. *Journal of Linguistics*, 22(2):411–437. Publisher: Cambridge University Press.

Lowit, A., Marchetti, A., Corson, S., and Kuschmann, A. (2018). Rhythmic performance in hypokinetic dysarthria: Relationship between reading, spontaneous speech and diadochokinetic tasks. *Journal of Communication Disorders*, 72:26–39.

Luce, P. A. and Pisoni, D. B. (1998). Recognizing Spoken Words: The Neighborhood Activation Model. *Ear and hearing*, 19(1):1–36.

MacGregor, L. J., Corley, M., and Donaldson, D. I. (2009). Not all disfluencies are are equal: The effects of disfluent repetitions on language comprehension. *Brain and Language*, 111(1):36–45.

Maekawa, K. (2003). Corpus of Spontaneous Japanese: Its design and evaluation. In *ISCA & IEEE Workshop on Spontaneous Speech Processing and Recognition*.

Maekawa, K. (2005). Toward a pronunciation dictionary of Japanese: Analysis of CSJ. In *Proceedings of Symposium on Large-Scale Knowledge Resources (LKR2005)*, pages 43–48.

Marslen-Wilson, W., Nix, A., and Gaskell, G. (1995). Phonological variation in lexical access: Abstractness, inference and english place assimilation. *Language and Cognitive Processes*, 10(3-4):285–308. Publisher: Routledge _eprint: https://doi.org/10.1080/01690969508407097.

Martin, J. G. and Strange, W. (1968). The perception of hesitation in spontaneous speech. *Perception & Psychophysics*, 3(6):427–438.

McAllister, J. (1991). The Processing of Lexically Stressed Syllables in Read and Spontaneous Speech. *Language and Speech*, 34(1): 1–26.

McAuliffe, M., Socolof, M., Mihuc, S., Wagner, M., and Sonderegger, M. (2017). Montreal Forced Aligner: Trainable Text-Speech Alignment Using Kaldi. In *Interspeech 2017*, pages 498–502. ISCA.

McClelland, J. L., Mirman, D., and Holt, L. L. (2006). Are there interactive processes in speech perception? *Trends in Cognitive Sciences*, 10(8):363–369.

McLennan, C. T., Luce, P. A., and Charles-Luce, J. (2003). Representation of lexical form. *Journal of Experimental Psychology: Learning, Memory, and Cognition*, 29(4):539–553.

McQueen, J. M. (2007). Eight questions about spoken word recognition. *The Oxford handbook of psycholinguistics*, pages 37–53.

McQueen, J. M., Norris, D., and Cutler, A. (2006). Are there really interactive processes in speech perception? *Trends in Cognitive Sciences*, 10(12):533. Publisher: Elsevier.

Megyesi, B. and Gustafson-Capkova, S. (2002). Production and Perception of Pauses and Their Linguistic Context in Read and Spontaneous Speech in Swedish. In *ICSLP 2002*, page 4, Denver, Colorado, USA.

Mehta, G. and Cutler, A. (1988). Detection of Target Phonemes in Spontaneous and Read Speech. *Language and Speech*, 31(2):135–156.

Meringer, R. and Mayer, C. (1895). *Versprechen und Verlesen: eine psychologisch-linguistische Studie*. G.I. Göschen'sche Verlagshandlung, Stuttgart.

Mitterer, H. and Ernestus, M. (2006). Listeners recover /t/s that speakers reduce: Evidence from /t/-lenition in Dutch. *Journal of Phonetics*, 34(1):73–103.

Mitterer, H. and McQueen, J. M. (2009). Processing reduced word-forms in speech perception using probabilistic knowledge about speech production. *Journal of Experimental Psychology. Human Perception and Performance*, 35(1):244–263.

Mitterer, H. and Tuinman, A. (2012). The Role of Native-Language Knowledge in the Perception of Casual Speech in a Second Language. *Frontiers in Psychology*, 3. Publisher: Frontiers.

Moniz, H., Batista, F., Mata, A. I., and Trancoso, I. (2014). Speaking style effects in the production of disfluencies. *Speech Communication*, 65: 20–35.

Mukai, Y. (2020). *Production and perception of reduced speech and the role of phonological-orthographic consistency*. Ph.D., University of Alberta, Edmonton, Alberta, Canada.

Mukai, Y. and Tucker, B. V. (2017). The phonetic reduction of nasals and voiced stops in Japanese across speech styles. In *Proceedings of the 31st General Meeting of the Phonetic Society of Japan*, pages 31–36, Tokyo. The Phonetic Society of Japan.

Munson, B. and Solomon, N. P. (2004). The Effect of Phonological Neighborhood Density on Vowel Articulation. *Journal of Speech, Language, and Hearing Research*, 47(5):1048–1058.

Nearey, T. M. (1995). A double-weak view of trading relations. *Papers in Laboratory phonology IV: Phonology and Phonetic Evidence*, pages 28–39.

Niedzielski, N. (1999). The Effect of Social Information on the Perception of Sociolinguistic Variables. *Journal of Language and Social Psychology*, 18(1):62 –85.

Norris, D. and McQueen, J. M. (2008). Shortlist B: a Bayesian model of continuous speech recognition. *Psychological Review*, 115(2):357–395.

Nosofsky, R. M. (1990). Relations between exemplar similarity and likelihood models of classification. *Journal of Mathematical Psychology*, 34:393–418.

Ochshorn, R. M. and Sloetjes, H. (2017). Gentle.

Oostdijk, N. (2000). The Spoken Dutch Corpus Project. *The ELRA Newsletter*, 5:4–8.

Papesh, M. H. and Goldinger, S. D. (2015). Pupillometry and Memory: External Signals of Metacognitive Control. In Gendolla, G. H., Tops, M., and Koole, S. L., editors, *Handbook of Biobehavioral Approaches to Self-Regulation*, pages 125–139. Springer, New York, NY.

Pickett, J. M. and Pollack, I. (1963). Intelligibility of Excerpts from Fluent Speech: Effects of Rate of Utterance and Duration of Excerpt. *Language and Speech*, 6(3):151–164.

Pitt, M. A. (2009). How are pronunciation variants of spoken words recognized? A test of generalization to newly learned words. *Journal of Memory and Language*, 61(1):19–36.

Pitt, M. A., Dilley, L., Johnson, K., Kiesling, S., Raymond, W., Hume, E., and Fosler-Lussier, E. (2007). Buckeye Corpus of Conversational Speech (2nd release)[http://www.buckeyecorpus.osu.edu] Columbus, OH: Department of Psychology. *Ohio State University (Distributor)*.

Plag, I., Homann, J., and Kunter, G. (2017). Homophony and morphology: The acoustics of word-final S in English 1. *Journal of Linguistics*, 53(1):181–216. Publisher: Cambridge University Press.

Pluymaekers, M., Ernestus, M., and Baayen, R. H. (2005a). Articulatory planning is continuous and sensitive to informational redundancy. *Phonetica*, 62:146–159.

Pluymaekers, M., Ernestus, M., and Baayen, R. H. (2005b). Lexical frequency and acoustic reduction in spoken Dutch. *The Journal of the Acoustical Society of America*, 118(4):2561–2569.

Podlubny, R. G., Nearey, T. M., Kondrak, G., and Tucker, B. V. (2018). Assessing the importance of several acoustic properties to the perception of spontaneous speech. *The Journal of the Acoustical Society of America*, 143(4):2255–2268.

Pollack, I. and Pickett, J. M. (1963). The Intelligibility of Excerpts from Conversation. *Language and Speech*, 6(3):165–171.

Pollack, I. and Pickett, J. M. (1964). Intelligibility of excerpts from fluent speech: Auditory vs. structural context. *Journal of Verbal Learning and Verbal Behavior*, 3(1):79–84.

Pols, L. C. W. (1996). Analysis and Perception of Dynamic Events and of Reduction Phenomena in Speech. In *ABSP-1996*, pages 17–22, Keele, England, UK. ISCA.

Prins, R. and Bastiaanse, R. (2004). Analyzing the spontaneous speech of aphasic speakers. *Aphasiology*, 18(12):1075–1091. Place: United Kingdom Publisher: Taylor & Francis.

Ranbom, L. J. and Connine, C. M. (2007). Lexical representation of phonological variation in spoken word recognition. *Journal of Memory and Language*, 57(2):273–298.

Rao, R. (2009). Deaccenting in Spontaneous Speech in Barcelona Spanish. *Studies in Hispanic and Lusophone Linguistics*, 2(1):31–76. Publisher: De Gruyter Mouton Section: Studies in Hispanic and Lusophone Linguistics.

Rapp, B., Buchwald, A., and Goldrick, M. (2014). Integrating accounts of speech production: the devil is in the representational details. *Language, Cognition and Neuroscience*, 29(1):24–27.

Raymond, W. D., Dautricourt, R., and Hume, E. (2006). Word-internal /t,d/ deletion in spontaneous speech: Modeling the effects of extra-linguistic, lexical, and phonological factors. *Language Variation and Change*, 18(1):55–97. Publisher: Cambridge University Press.

Renkema, J. (2009). *Discourse, of Course: An overview of research in discourse studies*. John Benjamins Publishing.

Renkema, J. and Schubert, C. (2018). *Introduction to Discourse Studies*. John Benjamins Publishing Company. Publication Title: z.219.

Roelofs, A. (2014). Integrating psycholinguistic and motor control approaches to speech production: where do they meet? *Language, Cognition and Neuroscience*, 29(1):35–37.

Saltzman, E. L. and Munhall, K. G. (1989). A Dynamical Approach to Gestural Patterning in Speech Production. *Ecological Psychology*, 1(4):333–382.

Samuel, A. G. (2011). Speech Perception. *Annual Review of Psychology*, 62(1):49–72. _eprint: https://doi.org/10.1146/annurev.psych.121208. 131643.

Schachter, S., Christenfeld, N., Ravina, B., and Bilous, F. (1991). Speech disfluency and the structure of knowledge. *Journal of Personality and Social Psychology*, 60(3):362–367. Place: US Publisher: American Psychological Association.

Schilling, N. (2013). Investigating Stylistic Variation. In *The Handbook of Language Variation and Change*, pages 325–349. John Wiley & Sons, Ltd.

Schnadt, M. J. and Corley, M. (2006). The Influence of Lexical, Conceptual and Planning Based Factors on Disfluency Production. *Proceedings of the Annual Meeting of the Cognitive Science Society*, 28(28).

Schuppler, B., Ernestus, M., Scharenborg, O., and Boves, L. (2011). Acoustic reduction in conversational Dutch: A quantitative analysis based on automatically generated segmental transcriptions. *Journal of Phonetics*, 39(1):96–109.

Schwab, S. and Avanzi, M. (2015). Regional variation and articulation rate in French. *Journal of Phonetics*, 48:96–105.

Shafaei-Bajestan, E., Moradipour-Tari, M., Uhrig, P., and Baayen, R. H. (2021). LDL-AURIS: a computational model, grounded in error-driven learning, for the comprehension of single spoken words. *Language, Cognition and Neuroscience*, 0(0):1–28. Publisher: Routledge _eprint: https://doi.org/10.1080/23273798.2021.1954207.

Shannon, C. E. (1948). A Mathematical Theory of Communication. *Bell System Technical Journal*, 27:379–423.

Shockey, L. (2008). *Sound Patterns of Spoken English*. John Wiley & Sons. Google-Books-ID: 9OWQGsOB62UC.

Shriberg, E. (2001). To 'errrr' is human: ecology and acoustics of speech disfluencies. *Journal of the International Phonetic Association*, 31(1):153–169. Publisher: Cambridge University Press.

Shriberg, E. (2005). Spontaneous speech: How people really talk and why engineers should care. In *Ninth European Conference on Speech Communication and Technology*.

Shriberg, E. E. (1994). *Preliminaries to a Theory of Speech Disfluencies*. PhD Thesis, University of California at Berkeley, Berkeley.

Sims, M. N. (2016). *The Role of Acoustic Detail in the Production and Processing of Vowels in Spontaneous Speech*. PhD Thesis, University of Alberta.

Smiljanić, R. and Bradlow, A. R. (2005). Production and perception of clear speech in Croatian and English. *The Journal of the Acoustical Society of America*, 118(3):1677–1688. Publisher: Acoustical Society of America.

Sonderegger, M., Bane, M., and Graff, P. (2017). The medium-term dynamics of accents on reality television. *Language*, 93(3):598–640. Publisher: Linguistic Society of America.

Steen, F. and Turner, M. (2021). Red Hen Lab.

Stemberger, J. P. (2017). Morphology in Language Production with Special Reference to Connectionism. In *The Handbook of Morphology*, pages 428–452. John Wiley & Sons, Ltd.

Story, B. H. (2005). A parametric model of the vocal tract area function for vowel and consonant simulation. *The Journal of the Acoustical Society of America*, 117(5):3231–3254. Publisher: Acoustical Society of America.

Sumner, M. (2013). A phonetic explanation of pronunciation variant effects. *The Journal of the Acoustical Society of America*, 134(1):EL26–EL32. Publisher: Acoustical Society of America.

Sumner, M. and Samuel, A. G. (2005). Perception and representation of regular variation: The case of final /t/. *Journal of Memory and Language*, 52(3):322–338.

Tang, K. and Bennett, R. (2018). Contextual predictability influences word and morpheme duration in a morphologically complex language (Kaqchikel Mayan). *The Journal of the Acoustical Society of America*, 144(2):997–1017. Publisher: Acoustical Society of America.

Taschenberger, L., Tuomainen, O., and Hazan, V. (2019). Disfluencies in spontaneous speech in easy and adverse communicative situations: The effect of age. In Rose, R. L. and Eklund, R., editors, *Proceedings of DiSS 2019*, pages 55–58, Budapest, Hungary. ELTE Faculty of Humanities.

Tily, H. and Kuperman, V. (2012). Rational phonological lengthening in spoken Dutch. *The Journal of the Acoustical Society of America*, 132(6):3935–3940. Publisher: Acoustical Society of America.

Tomaschek, F., Plag, I., Ernestus, M., and Baayen, R. H. (2021a). Phonetic effects of morphology and context: Modeling the duration of word-final S in English with naïve discriminative learning. *Journal of Linguistics*, 57(1):123–161. Publisher: Cambridge University Press.

Tomaschek, F. and Tucker, B. V. (2021). The role of coarticulatory acoustic detail in the perception of verbal inflection. *JASA Express Letters*, 1(8):085201.

Tomaschek, F., Tucker, B. V., Ramscar, M., and Harald Baayen, R. (2021b). Paradigmatic enhancement of stem vowels in regular English inflected verb forms. *Morphology*, 31(2):171–199.

Tomasello, M. and Stahl, D. (2004). Sampling children's spontaneous speech: how much is enough? *Journal of Child Language*, 31(1):101–121. Publisher: Cambridge University Press.

Torreira, F., Adda-Decker, M., and Ernestus, M. (2010). The Nijmegen Corpus of Casual French. *Speech Communication*, 52(3):201–212.

Trouvain, J., Koreman, J., Erriquez, A., and Braun, B. (2001). Articulation Rate Measures and Their Relation to Phone Classification in Spontaneous and Read German Speech. In *Proceedings of the 16th International Congress of the Phonetic Sciences*, pages 155–158.

Tucker, B. V. (2007). Processing of fine phonetic detail in American English flaps. In *Journal of the Acoustical Society of America*, volume 121, page 3170.

Tucker, B. V. (2011). The effect of reduction on the processing of flaps and /g/ in isolated words. *Journal of Phonetics*, 39(3):312–318.

Tucker, B. V., Brenner, D., Danielson, D. K., Kelley, M. C., Nenadić, F., and Sims, M. (2019a). The Massive Auditory Lexical Decision (MALD) database. *Behavior Research Methods*, 51(3):1187–1204.

Tucker, B. V. and Ernestus, M. (2016). Why we need to investigate casual speech to truly understand language production, processing and the mental lexicon. *The Mental Lexicon*, 11(3):375–400.

Tucker, B. V., Sims, M., and Baayen, R. H. (2019b). Opposing forces on acoustic duration. Technical report, PsyArXiv.

Tucker, B. V. and Warner, N. (2007). Inhibition of processing due to reduction of the American English flap. In *Proceedings of the 16th International Congress of the Phonetic Sciences*, pages 1949–1952.

Tucker, B. V. and Wright, R. (2020). Introduction to the special issue on the phonetics of under-documented languages. *The Journal of the Acoustical Society of America*, 147(4):2741–2744. Publisher: Acoustical Society of America.

Tuinman, A., Mitterer, H., and Cutler, A. (2012). Resolving ambiguity in familiar and unfamiliar casual speech. *Journal of Memory and Language*, 66(4):530–544.

Turnbull, R. (2018). Patterns of probabilistic segment deletion/reduction in English and Japanese. *Linguistics Vanguard*, 4(s2). Publisher: De Gruyter Section: Linguistics Vanguard.

Uchanski, R. M. (2005). Clear Speech. In *The Handbook of Speech Perception*, pages 207–235. John Wiley & Sons, Ltd. Section: 9 _eprint: https://onlinelibrary.wiley.com/doi/pdf/10.1002/9780470757024.ch9.

Van de Ven, M. and Ernestus, M. (2018). The role of segmental and durational cues in the processing of reduced words. *Language and Speech*, 61(3):358–383.

Van de Ven, M., Ernestus, M., and Schreuder, R. (2012). Predicting acoustically reduced words in spontaneous speech: The role of semantic/syntactic and acoustic cues in context. *Laboratory Phonology*, 3(2):455–481. Publisher: De Gruyter Section: Laboratory Phonology.

Van de Ven, M., Tucker, B. V., and Ernestus, M. (2010). Semantic facilitation in bilingual everyday speech comprehension. In *Proceedings of the 11th Annual Conference of the International Speech Communication Association*, pages 1245–1248.

Van de Ven, M., Tucker, B. V., and Ernestus, M. (2011). Semantic context effects in the comprehension of reduced pronunciation variants. *Memory & Cognition*, 39(7):1301–1316.

van den Oord, A., Dieleman, S., Zen, H., Simonyan, K., Vinyals, O., Graves, A., Kalchbrenner, N., Senior, A., and Kavukcuoglu, K. (2016). WaveNet: A Generative Model for Raw Audio. *arXiv:1609.03499 [cs]*. arXiv: 1609.03499.

Van Engen, K. J., Baese-Berk, M., Baker, R. E., Choi, A., Kim, M., and Bradlow, A. R. (2010). The Wildcat Corpus of Native-and Foreign-accented English: Communicative Efficiency across Conversational Dyads with Varying Language Alignment Profiles. *Language and Speech*, 53(4):510–540.

van Son, R., Koopmans-van Beinum, F., and Pols, L. C. W. (1998). Efficiency As An Organizing Principle Of Natural Speech. In *ICSLP-1998*, page 0203, Sydney, Australia.

Vance, T. J. (2008). *The Sounds of Japanese with Audio CD*. Cambridge University Press.

VanDam, M., Warlaumont, A. S., Bergelson, E., Cristia, A., Soderstrom, M., De Palma, P., and MacWhinney, B. (2016). HomeBank: An Online Repository of Daylong Child-Centered Audio Recordings. *Seminars in speech and language*, 37(2):128–142.

Vaughan, N., Storzbach, D., and Furukawa, I. (2006). Sequencing versus Nonsequencing Working Memory in Understanding of Rapid Speech by Older Listeners. *Journal of the American Academy of Audiology*, 17(07):506–518. Publisher: American Academy of Audiology.

Wagner, P., Trouvain, J., and Zimmerer, F. (2015). In defense of stylistic diversity in speech research. *Journal of Phonetics*, 48:1–12.

Ward, W. (1989). Understanding Spontaneous Speech. In *Speech and Natural Language: Proceedings of a Workshop Held at Philadelphia, Pennsylvania, February 21-23, 1989*.

Warner, N. (2011). Reduction. In van Oostendorp, M., Ewen, C., Hume, E., and Rice, K., editors, *The Blackwell Companion to Phonology: General issues and segmental phonology*, volume 1, pages 1866–1891. John Wiley & Sons.

Warner, N. (2012). Methods for studying spontaneous speech. In *The Oxford Handbook of Laboratory Phonology*, pages 621–633. Oxford University Press, Oxford.

Warner, N., Fountain, A., and Tucker, B. V. (2009). Cues to perception of reduced flaps. *The Journal of the Acoustical Society of America*, 125(5):3317–3327. Publisher: Acoustical Society of America.

Warner, N. and Park, S. (2018). Spontaneous speech in the teaching of phonetics and speech perception. In *ISAPh 2018 International Symposium on Applied Phonetics*, pages 32–38. ISCA.

Warner, N. and Tucker, B. V. (2011). Phonetic variability of stops and flaps in spontaneous and careful speech. *The Journal of the Acoustical Society of America*, 130(3):1606–1617.

Weber, A. and Scharenborg, O. (2012). Models of spoken-word recognition. *Wiley Interdisciplinary Reviews: Cognitive Science*, 3(3):387–401.

Wenke, R. J., Cornwell, P., and Theodoros, D. G. (2010). Changes to articulation following LSVT® and traditional dysarthria therapy in non-progressive dysarthria. *International Journal of Speech-Language Pathology*, 12(3):203–220. Publisher: Taylor & Francis _eprint: https://doi.org/10.3109/17549500903568468.

Wickham, H. (2016). *ggplot2: Elegant Graphics for Data Analysis*. Springer-Verlag New York.

Wieling, M., Grieve, J., Bouma, G., Fruehwald, J., Coleman, J., and Liberman, M. (2016). Variation and Change in the Use of Hesitation Markers in Germanic Languages. *Language Dynamics and Change*, 6(2):199–234. Publisher: Brill Section: Language Dynamics and Change.

Winn, M. B., Wendt, D., Koelewijn, T., and Kuchinsky, S. E. (2018). Best Practices and Advice for Using Pupillometry to Measure Listening Effort: An Introduction for Those Who Want to Get Started. *Trends in Hearing*, 22:233121651880086.

Wright, R. (2004). Factors of lexical competition in vowel articulation. In Local, J., Ogden, R., and R, T., editors, *Papers in Laboratory Phonology 6*, pages 75–87. Cambridge University Press, Cambridge.

Xu, Y. (2010). In defense of lab speech. *Journal of Phonetics*, 38(3):329–336.

Yuan, J., Lai, W., Cieri, C., and Liberman, M. (2018). Using Forced Alignment for Phonetics Research. *Chinese Language Resources and Processing: Text, Speech and Language Technology*.

Yuan, J. and Liberman, M. (2008). Speaker identification on the SCOTUS corpus. *Proceedings of Acoustics '08*, pages 5687–5690.

Zekveld, A. A., Kramer, S. E., and Festen, J. M. (2010). Pupil Response as an Indication of Effortful Listening: The Influence of Sentence Intelligibility. *Ear and Hearing*, 31(4):480–490.

Zellers, M., Schuppler, B., and Clayards, M. (2018). Introduction, or: why rethink reduction? In Cangemi, F., Clayards, M., Niebuhr, O., Schuppler, B., and Zellers, M., editors, *Rethinking reduction*, pages 1–23. De Gruyter Mouton. Publisher: de Gruyter Mouton Berlin.

Zevin, J. D. and Balota, D. A. (2000). Priming and attentional control of lexical and sublexical pathways during naming. *Journal of Experimental Psychology: Learning, Memory, and Cognition*, 26(1):121–135. Place: US Publisher: American Psychological Association.

Zimmerer, F. and Reetz, H. (2014). Do listeners recover "deleted" final /t/ in German? *Frontiers in Psychology*, 5. Publisher: Frontiers.

Zipf, G. K. (1949). *Human Behavior and the Principle of the Least Effort. An Introduction to Human Ecology*. Hafner, New York.

Zue, V., Seneff, S., and Glass, J. (1990). Speech database development at MIT: Timit and beyond. *Speech Communication*, 9(4):351–356.

Zue, V. W. and Laferriere, M. (1979). Acoustic study of medial /t,d/ in American English. *The Journal of the Acoustical Society of America*, 66(4):1039–1050.

Zwitserlood, P. (2018). Processing and Representation of Morphological Complexity in Native Language Comprehension and Production. In Booij, G., editor, *The Construction of Words: Advances in Construction Morphology*, Studies in Morphology, pages 583–602. Springer International Publishing, Cham.

Acknowledgments

The authors would like to thank: Catherine Ford, Matthew C. Kelley, Kaidi Lõo, Gabrielle Morin, Filip Nenadić, Scott James Perry, Fabian Tomaschek, M.J. Tucker, and Richard Wright for discussion and feedback while writing and developing this overview. We would also like to thank David Deterding and two anonymous reviewers for their comments and feedback on earlier versions of this overview. Any errors or missing content are of course our own.

Cambridge Elements ☰

Phonetics

David Deterding
Universiti Brunei Darussalam

David Deterding is a Professor at Universiti Brunei Darussalam. His research has involved the measurement of rhythm, description of the pronunciation of English in Singapore, Brunei and China, and the phonetics of Austronesian languages such as Malay, Brunei Malay, and Dusun.

Advisory Board

About the Series

The Cambridge Elements in Phonetics series will generate a range of high-quality scholarly works, offering researchers and students authoritative accounts of current knowledge and research in the various fields of phonetics. In addition, the series will provide detailed descriptions of research into the pronunciation of a range of languages and language varieties. There will be elements describing the phonetics of the major languages of the world, such as French, German, Chinese and Malay as well as the pronunciation of endangered languages, thus providing a valuable resource for documenting and preserving them.

Cambridge Elements ≡

Phonetics

Elements in the Series

The Phonetics of Malay
David Deterding, Ishamina Athirah Gardiner, Najib Noorashid

Spontaneous Speech
Benjamin V. Tucker, Yoichi Mukai

A full series listing is available at: www.cambridge.org/EIPH

Printed in the United States
by Baker & Taylor Publisher Services